LUMBERJACK SKY PILOT

by
Frank A. Reed

North Country Books
Utica, New York

LUMBERJACK SKY PILOT

Copyright © 1965
by Frank A. Reed

FIRST EDITION
FOURTH PRINTING, 2007

ISBN-10: 0-925168-81-5
ISBN-13: 978-0-925168-81-8

John D. Mahaffy, *Art Director*
Harold W. Charbonneau, *Production Manager*

John D. Mahaffy, *cover art 2001*

Original Printing by
Willard Press, Boonville, New York

NORTH COUNTRY BOOKS, INC.
311 Turner Street
Utica, New York 13501

www.northcountrybooks.com

This book is dedicated to the memory of old-time lumberjacks in the Northeast and the Lake States who worked in the forest with great skill, energy and dedication to supply wood products for the happiness of people, the strength of the nation and the glory of God.

PREFACE

As publishers, all books that we publish are important to us, but every once in a while there is that "special one" that we are particularly proud of for one reason or another. *Lumberjack Sky Pilot* is one of those.

When I recently spoke to John Mahaffy, one of the original founders of North Country Books, about our reprinting *Lumberjack*, the first thing he said was that it is a "very special book" for him, and it is. After all, it was the book that launched North Country Books into regional publishing some thirty-six years ago.

Frank Reed had written *Lumberjack Sky Pilot* and needed a publisher. His friends, Bill Charbonneau and John Mahaffy, owned a printing business, and John was a talented graphic artist to boot.

Frank Reed's story of life in the lumber camps of the North Country depicts the experiences of Aaron Maddox, Charles Atwood, Clarence Mason and Reed, himself, in the Adirondacks; and also includes William Burger of Northern New England and Frank Higgins of Minnesota.

It is our hope that by reprinting this North Country classic, a new generation of Adirondack lovers will have the opportunity to read these recollections and have a glimpse into the lives of the men in the lumber camps and of the sky pilots.

In memory of Frank Reed and Bill Charbonneau, this is an exact reprint of the first text edition.

—Sheila Orlin
Publisher

TABLE OF CONTENTS

ILLUSTRATIONS

I

FRANK HIGGINS

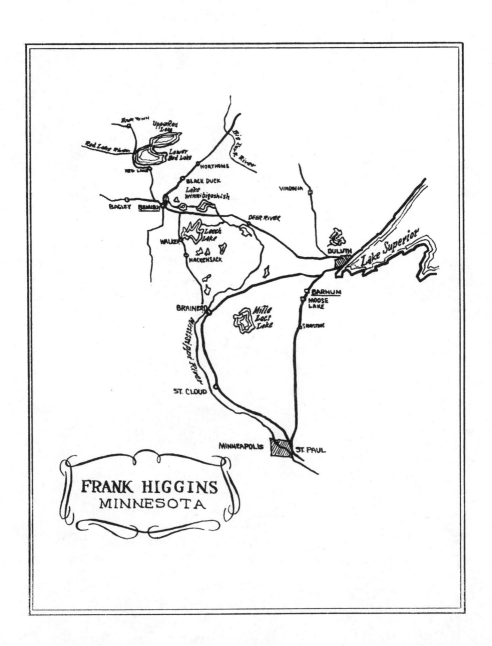

FRANK HIGGINS
MINNESOTA

2

Frank Higgins

Early Life in Ontario

Frank Higgins was the pioneer sky pilot, the one who laid the foundation for the work of other men. He visited his first lumber camp near Barnum, Minnesota, in 1895, and, within ten years, was a national figure as sky pilot to the lumberjacks.

Frank was born in a hotel operated by his father at Toronto, Ontario, on August 19, 1865, the youngest in a family of seven children. His father died when Frank was seven years of age, leaving the mother to care for a large family. Two years later she married an Englishman by the name of John Castle, and the family moved westward to settle on a homestead at Shelburne, Ontario.

Children in the homesteader's family had to work much of the year in clearing the land, preparing the soil for planting and in cultivating and harvesting the crops. They had opportunity for school only in the winter season after the crops had been gathered in. Frank's educational opportunities were limited by the hard work on the homestead and the short school term. He gave up school at the end of the fifth grade.

However his work on the farm was laying foundations for the future in unexpected ways. He built strength and skill by his long hours of labor in the field and forest. His skill with the axe, the saw, the file and the grindstone were particularly valuable to him in his later years of service in the Minnesota forest.

A somewhat revolutionary religious experience when he was eighteen years of age gave the young and sturdy homesteader a deep appreciation of spiritual values and a desire to enter the Christian ministry. The need for more education was evident if he was to pursue that desire. He entered the sixth grade of the public school at Toronto, in 1885, when he was at the age of twenty and continued his studies there for the next five years when he completed his work as a high school sophomore.

Frank preached for a while in a Methodist church at Annondale, Minnesota, but soon came under the care of the Presbytery of Duluth which advised him on his preparation for the ministry and his service in that field. He entered Hameline University at St. Paul, Minnesota, in the early autumn of 1893 for a two year period of study.

3

The Presbytery of Duluth observed the growth and progress of the young student for the ministry and appointed him as a student supply at Barnum, Minnesota, when he had completed the term of study in June, 1895, and was thirty years of age. The church at Barnum had been built five years before to serve the lumbermen and a growing number of farmers in the area.

Mrs. Herman Gurlock of Duluth, who was then Miss Clara Anderson, arrived in Barnum on the same Sunday that Frank Higgins conducted his first service and later became the church organist. She told the writer the story of anticipation on the part of the congregation and the enthusiasm of the people for the new minister who was a large, muscular man with loud voice for both singing and speaking, sincere purpose and great dedication to the service of God and the people.

His service in the church at Barnum was so effective that the congregation requested his continuation as the supply pastor. His ministry there was a very fruitful one which deserved recognition in its own right.

Preaching in the Lumber Camps

However, his service at Barnum was more strategic as the opening of a larger ministry which began in this manner. The Barnum church had an officer by the name of Martin Cain, who was both a lumber manufacturer and a big logging operator. He had several camps operating in the area and particularly in the Kettle River section and took Frank Higgins along on one of his trips.

At one of the Kettle River driving camps, the men were eating an outdoor lunch when Frank and Mr. Cain arrived. After a few minutes conversation with his foreman, Mr. Cain turned to the crew and said, "Boys, this big fellow is Frank Higgins. He is our pastor at the church in Barnum. When you are in town some Sunday come and hear him."

The lumberjacks looked Higgins over, admired the width of his shoulders, and one of them said, "A preacher, huh? All right, preacher, give us a sermon." Frank was somewhat taken aback and replied, "I'm sorry, boys, but I have no Bible and no notes with me."

Quite seriously the lumberjack said, "It's a sorry preacher who doesn't have at least ONE sermon in his heart."

Frank nodded in agreement and added, "Lad, you're right." He climbed up on a stump, recalled as best he could the sermon of the preceding day, and gave them the best that was in him. The men listened with rapt attention while Frank told them about "The Friend of Sinners." Before he was half way through, the men were so quiet they seem-

4

ed almost to have stopped breathing. When the sermon ended, Frank bowed his head and prayed for each man, for his home and family, and for his final salvation. One by one they came up to shake his hand and thank him for his words.

This trip with Martin Cain to the Kettle River camp opened a great door of opportunity. As word went round to other camps, he was invited to others also, until after a time, he was making the rounds of several lumber camps in the area along with the work of the church at Barnum.

One night as a crew sat in camp, the lumberjacks were drying their clothes around the great stove, and Frank was talking to them in an informal way about the consequences of sin and the way of escape. One of the lumberjacks asked, "Preacher, what is your greatest ambition in life?" Frank answered, "To pilot men to the skies!" The lumberjack said in all seriousness, "Well, you ought to make a good 'sky pilot;' you seem to know the way." The name stuck, and before many years the whole Christian world knew about the Sky Pilot of the north woods.

Another man in the camp that night made this additional comment. "In these woods there are thirty thousand men, and I'll bet not more than thirty of them hear a sermon a year on the average."

Frank held his breath with amazement and asked, "How many men did you say work in the woods?"

"Thirty thousand."

"And they never hear the Gospel?"

"No sir, they do not. How can they?"

"Well, they're going to" Frank concluded, "even if I have to tell it to every one of them myself."

So the great idea was born, and an epic of evangelism began. Frank went back to Barnum and talked with Martin Cain and his fellows, and they enthusiastically encouraged him.

Frank Higgins had been married to Eva Lucas on Oct. 9, 1897, and took her to the manse in Barnum. His ministry in the parish at Barnum and the wider parish in neighboring lumber camps was a successful and challenging one which apparently was to continue for some years had it not been for an unusual event which took place in the community.

The Dying Lumberjack's Challenge

One cold winter day in 1899 he was called to the home of a logger who had been brought out from camp to his humble home in the edge of the village, seriously ill. The village doctor, who was already there when Higgins arrived, called him aside and said, "I don't think we can

5

help him here. If he could be gotten to the hospital in Duluth, there might be some chance." Higgins replied, "I will go with him to the hospital."

A short time afterwards the man was carefully wrapped, laid in a sleigh on a stretcher and taken to the railroad station, where he was transferred to the baggage car and rode in the baggage car with Higgins as his companion to the city of Duluth. There he was taken to a hospital by ambulance.

After the hospital doctors had given him a careful examination, one of them called Higgins aside and advised, "I am sorry but there isn't much hope for your man's life. Perhaps you will want to tell him." Thinking the man might want at least to make some provision for his family, Frank Higgins imparted this information carefully and kindly.

To his surprise, the man looked up into his face with a smile and said: "Mr. Higgins, I am so glad you came to our camp one evening some weeks ago. I was brought up in a Christian home back east. I attended the church and the Sunday School as a boy, but, since boyhood, I have been working in the woods and hadn't attended a religious service for more than 20 years.

"Your service in the bunkhouse that night brought back old memories out of the past. After you were gone and the lights were out, I knelt down by my bunk and gave myself again to God in Christ.

"Now, I am going home. I can't do anything for my fellow lumberjacks, but you can. They need you more than the churches do. Go back and tell them the old story that Christ can make them live."

A short time afterwards, this logger passed from the scene of this life and was laid at rest with tender care by Frank Higgins three days later. However, his dying words continued to live and burn their way deeper into the mind and soul of Frank Higgins. They burned there both day and night until, at the end of some weeks, he resigned as minister of the church and dedicated his life to service in the Minnesota logging camps.

Move to Bemiji, Minnesota

A part of the call to larger service came in an opportunity at Bemiji, which was in the heart of a great logging area farther west where logging activities in the neighboring pine forests were greatly on the increase. The move included service for a while in a new parish where the first minister had found it impossible to remain.

When Higgins arrived in Bemiji, he found that the liquor and gambling elements were dominant in the town. The church had few members and was not a potent force in the life of the community. He set about changing that situation.

6

One day soon after his arrival, Frank Higgins was standing on a street corner when a flashily dressed man approached and asked, "Who are you?"

"I am the new minister here," Higgins replied.

"Well you won't last long here" retorted the stranger. "We drove the other men out. You will have to go also. When doctors hit the town, folks die; when ministers come, folks go to hell. We will clear you out pretty damned quick."

"I guess it's my play," said Higgins. "Here's where I serve notice I intend to stay." The closed fist of Higgins landed heavily on the chin of the gambler, and he in turn landed heavily in the muddy gutter.

The town marshal hurried forward to inquire what was wrong with Higgins. He replied, "Nothing wrong with me; there seems to be something wrong with the man down there in the gutter."

This incident helped to make the liquor and gambling interests aware that in Frank Higgins they had an adversary who was not easily discouraged or afraid to fight. His service in the community included the completion of the new church building and a successful movement to lift the level of spiritual and moral life in the community. A daughter, Marguerite, came to gladden the Higgins home early in their Bimiji ministry.

He followed the pattern he had set at Barnum, preaching in his pulpit on Sunday, and spending the week in camps. At first he was greeted with amazement and some suspicion, as the men could not believe that any person had an unselfish purpose in seeking them and sharing their dangers and discomforts. Altruism was a quality a lumberjack rarely met. But as the weeks passed and the men learned to admire and respect the short giant who entered their work, their sport, their sorrows, and their troubles the way became easy. His visits were eagerly awaited, and when his stocky form appeared trudging down a toteroad with his knapsack on his back, the whole camp welcomed him. In his knapsack he carried a few necessities and a load of Bibles, song-books, reading material and small comforts for the men. Many a stout fellow "hefted" that pack and marveled that any man could carry it mile after mile. Indeed, it was the great weight of that heavy "turkey" which finally caused the sky pilot's death.

The church at Bemiji proved an ideal base for the camp work, and weeks went by during which the town saw the pastor only on Sundays. The woods claimed six-sevenths of his time. When winter settled down, the sky pilot put on snowshoes and continued his rounds. When the snow packed, he changed to skis, and dragged a toboggan behind him, on which he transported his familiar load of Bibles, hymnals, and litera-

7

ture. Then one day a man, desperately sick, had to be taken from a camp to the hospital, and Frank dragged him on the toboggan over the crusted snows. The trip was so hard that the sky pilot realized he had to have some means of transportation, and set his mind to solve this problem. He hit upon the idea of training a dog team, and out of Bemiji in a short time he operated the first dog-drawn ambulance the woodsmen had ever seen or heard of.

With this aid the preacher could increase his weight of supplies, so he was able to stay out longer and travel farther from his base. When the spring came he retired his dogs to a well-earned rest. Many a sick or injured lumberjack rode "outside" to a hospital and adequate medical aid behind those missionary dogs, and many an expectant mother made the same trip in safety and comfort. Doing enough work to kill two ordinary men, the Little Giant thrived and rejoiced in his original ministry, and his name became a legend among the lumberjacks. Whenever he went into a strange camp or into new territory, he needed only to announce his name, and respectful attention was accorded him. The sheer manhood and virility of the preacher were his passport among the strong men and his loving heart was the key which unlocked every door he wished to enter.

As time passed it became evident to Frank Higgins and the church people that he could not carry the increasing work of the church and the rapidly developing work in the lumber camps. He resigned as supply pastor of the Bemiji church and devoted his full time and energy to his ministry in the lumber camps.

A Famous Criminal Turns Sky Pilot

On one of his camp visits, Frank Higgins met a man by the name of John who appeared to have a peculiar background. At the service in the bunkhouse that evening Higgins told the story of the Prodigal Son including his journey into the far country, the riotous living, his desperate condition when his money was gone, his return to the old home, the father's reception and the feast with the fat calf.

As Higgins progressed in the story he observed the look on John's face which was at first scornful and then seemed to change. After the service he conferred with John outside and told him more of the story of God's love and forgiveness through Christ. Higgins told the story so effectively that it burned its way into the mind and heart of John and he became a follower of Christ that night. He was one of the twice-born men.

Just as Higgins became aware of a spiritual revolution which was taking place in the life of a Minnesota lumberjack, he asked the name of

8

his new found friend. John asked, "Did you ever hear of Jack McWilliams? I am he."

This was startling news to even a sky pilot. Jack McWilliams was the most wanted criminal in Minnesota. He had been a prize fighter but had become a drunkard which led him into all sorts of other sins including murder. Every officer in the state of Minnesota was on the lookout for Jack McWilliams.

Jack's religious experience turned out to be a sound conversion. He soon began to give his testimony in the camp.

Jack thought perhaps he should give himself up to the authorities but Higgins advised against it as he had other plans. When Higgins made the logging operator aware of the conversion of Jack McWilliams, Mr. Ward made Jack an assistant foreman in a remote camp where he could work with vigor in the woods and lead a religious service on Sunday. Sometimes Frank Higgins also had him share in the religious service at that and neighboring camps.

One day Frank Higgins went to the state capital in St. Paul. Next day he sent a telegram which Mr. Ward delivered to Jack at the camp. It read, "I am in a jam in St. Paul trying to help a friend. Will you come and help me?"

Jack made ready his pack and rode with Mr. Ward to the railroad station. He arrived some hours later in Minneapolis with a beard of several months growth. Frank met him at the train and said, "Don't ask any questions right now, but do as I tell you and I'll explain later. You look wild enough to scare yourself! Go get a haircut, a shave, a massage, a bath, and a good suit of clothes and come to my hotel."

Jack got what the boys called "the works" at the barber shop, bought some new clothes, and even got a handkerchief with some perfume on it to finish up the job. Frank was delighted with his civilized appearance, and asked him if he had ever been in St. Paul. John said he had been there when he was in the ring, but didn't know much about the city. The wily Higgins said, "Well, we are going over there now and get in touch with some pretty important people, and see if they can help this friend of mine. You follow my lead and answer any questions they ask you."

When they were near the capital, Frank said, "John, here is where we make our first call. Stick close to me and do just as I tell you." They entered the capital, went down a long hall, and entered a waiting room where several people were waiting. Frank went up to a secretary seated at a desk and said, "Mr. Day, this is the man we were talking about." The secretary replied, "Hello, Higgins, the Governor is expecting you, you

9

are to walk right in. He said to give you precedence over anyone else who might be waiting."

It was not until they were in the governor's office that John knew what had happened. He felt trapped, and looked around for a way out, but all the doors were closed, the windows were too high to reach, and he saw that he was unable to either fight or run. He trusted Higgins, and knew that if he was delivering a friend to the law, it was the best thing to do.

After a few minutes of conversation the governor smiled with pleasure, put his arm around the outlaw and said, "John, I feel happy and honored to know you, not because of what you were, but because of what you have become. Never go back on the God who has done so much for all of us in and through the cross of His Son!" Then turning to the sky pilot, he said, "Mr. Higgins, I am convinced. This man is really converted. Nothing but the power of God Almighty can put before our eyes a man like this, but I have a duty as a Christian which means more than my political career. I am going to give this man a full and complete pardon, and leave him free to serve the Savior."

Governor Johnson stepped to his desk, wrote and signed a full pardon for John Sornberger, alias Jack McWilliams, and John was a free man. He wept with joy, and the governor, deeply moved, put one arm around Frank and the other around John, and said, "Boys let us pray!" And the governor of the state knelt in his office, with his arm around the noted sky pilot, and the most dreaded outlaw of the realm, and committed them both to the Grace of God. Rising to their feet the governor said, "Write to me, John, and come and see me often. I'll be interested in knowing how you get along, and in hearing about your career as a preacher." John promised and they left the executive's office.

As the demands grew for services in the lumber camps over a wider area in Minnesota, it became evident that one man could not carry the complete responsibility for a parish that was two hundred miles square, and populated by thirty thousand men, especially when most of the traveling had to be done on foot or by canoe, in rain, snow, ice and sleet, and in temperatures which varied between 90 degrees above zero to 50 degrees below. To his aid he called other giants of the spirit, each of them a stalwart in his own right. Some of these assistant pilots were men who had found Christ through Frank's efforts, and any and all of them were devoted to his interests. He had the native ability to bind men to him in loyalty and affection, as his own spirit stirred a response in those who became acquainted with him. The lumberjacks called all of these men "sky pilots," and when they had been a month in the camps it would have been

10

hard to tell the preacher from the crew! They shared the lives and hardships of the men of their wild parish, and did heroic services for God.

Among these early colleagues were such men as Fred Davis, Jack McCall, Matt Daly, Pete Peterson, John Sornberger, John McGinnis, Dick Farrell, and Al Channer. Dick Farrell, like John Sornberger, was an ex-pugilist and every one of this group was capable of giving a good account of himself in a brawl. But they avoided trouble when they could. Their purpose was to preach Christ, not to win fights—although none of them ever ran from trouble of any sort. Out of this group Frank formed the famed "Shanty Men's Association," and under this name the company went forth to spread the Gospel over the north woods.

No offerings were taken in the lumber camps. Frank Higgins raised money by speaking in churches and other places to pay the salaries of men and a small amount for travelling expenses.

Higgins as a National Figure

As the news of his work in the lumber camps spread far beyond the limits of the Minnesota forest, he was asked to address the General Assembly of the Presbyterian Church which was held that year in Atlantic City, New Jersey. People who were in attendance at that General Assembly have told the writer that the outstanding address of that Assembly was made by Frank Higgins. He had such a profound effect upon Commissioners at the Assembly and Board members that his work was adopted by the Board of Home Missions and became a vital part of its program. He was appointed by the Board as Director of Religious Work in the lumber camps throughout the United States.

As the news of his parish in the Minnesota pines spread over a wider area, Frank Higgins was called on to speak in churches and many other places as well as in the camps. As a result of this increased effort on his part, additional funds became available to carry on the work of his associates in the lumber camp parish.

His daughter Marguarite (now Mrs. Wesley A. Scheer) who lives at Howard Lake, Minnesota, has supplied the writer with a copy of her father's itinerary in the autumn of 1910. This autumn journey included addresses in such widely separated cities as Ann Arbor, Michigan; Columbus, Ohio; Wilmington, Delaware; Baltimore. Maryland; Philadelphia, Pennsylvania; New York City; Babylon, Long Island; Albany and Buffalo, New York, between October 9 and December 4. This was part of an effort on his part to supply the demand in the cities and villages for information on the Minnesota lumberjack.

However, Frank Higgins' heart was in the camps and he spent as much time as possible in them, bringing the gospel to them as the dying lumberjack in the Duluth hospital had advised him to do. He also visited other logging areas where religious services might be held in the camps. These journeys led him to lumber camps in Montana, Oregon, Idaho, Washington and California where many of his former Minnesota lumberjacks were at work.

Frank Higgins visited the Adirondack Mountains in Northern New York in the winter of 1912-13 and spent about three weeks in the lumber camps there. During that period, he conducted religious services in places where they had never been held before and preached the gospel of Christ to many men who never heard the story. He saw that there were in the Adirondacks several thousand men who had little contact with the church of any denomination.

The Adirondack journey included a trip with Rev. A. W. Maddox, who was a pastor in Tupper Lake, to the camps of the Santa Clara Lumber Company on the Cold River which is a branch of the Raquette River. Frank Eldred, who now lives in Tupper Lake, took him with a team on part of the journey.

His trip also included visits to a number of lumber camps along the Adirondack Division of the New York Central and especially those around Woods Lake. He was a speaker at churches in Tupper Lake and Old Forge.

At the close of his Adirondack visit, he met with a group of key men from the Synod of New York in Utica, made a report on his visit and recommended the establishment of a parish in the Adirondack lumber camps. The men accepted his recommendation and made plans for the establishment of the parish on January 1, 1914. Synodical Superintendent U. L. Mackey was a prime mover in adopting the program.

The story of an event which took place one day in Duluth, Minnesota, shows interesting insight into Frank Higgins' nature.

When he had been the sky pilot for a few years and fame had already come to him, he was in Duluth on a visit. He was in company with a friend named Charles Goodell, who at that time was a business man of some consequences. As the two men strolled down Superior Street, a third man accosted them and spoke to Mr. Goodell. After a few words together, Mr. Goodell said to his friend, "Gus, I'd like you to meet Frank Higgins."

As they shook hands, Gus said, "This is not *the* Frank Higgins, the Sky Pilot, is it?"

Frank smiled and admitted his identity, whereupon Gus said, "Mr. Higgins, I have wanted to meet you ever since I first heard of your great

12

work. I have also wished I could hear you preach. Indeed, I'd go any distance to hear a sermon from you."

Frank asked, "Do you mean that?"

Gus answered, "You bet I do!"

"Allright," Frank said, "take off your hat, you are in church!" He stepped off the curb, turned to face the sidewalk, took his pocket Bible out and read a text to his audience of two men. Then in his great voice he started to preach. Three men passing by stopped to listen, five more joined them, and in a few minutes scores of men were crowded around listening to the message of the Cross. For years after that Mr. Goodell was fond of telling the episode, and Gus *never* forgot it! He found Christ in that sermon.

His Illness and Death

As Frank Higgins' fruitful ministry in the lumber camps of Minnesota came toward the end of two decades, a cloud of ill health overshadowed his future. He had battled storm and cold, carrying seventy-five pounds in his pack, and the irritation of the pack-straps across his shoulders finally produced a spot so sore he realized he must have medical attention and entered the hospital at Rochester, Minnesota. The surgeon diagnosed the case as sarcoma, brought on by the constant weight of the pack. He advised an immediate operation, as the case was far advanced, and he held out small hope of a complete recovery. Frank decided at once to submit to the operation, which was performed on April 16, 1914.

The patient was very slow to rally, and the doctors, greatly concerned, decided upon a series of blood transfusions. A call went out, and in a few hours a delegation of eight rough men appeared at the hospital. They stated that they were lumberjacks who had come to give their blood for the man who had given his life to them. The leader said, "If there ain't blood enough in us eight men, say the word and every man in Northern Minnesota will be on his way down here tomorrow!"

Another delegate said, "Doc, if Frank Higgins needs blood, meat, or bones, I'll get a thousand men here in twenty-four hours for you to whittle on!" And he meant it. He spoke sober and restrained truth.

The sky pilot made a slow recovery, and after a number of weeks they told him, "Your days are numbered, and the number is small. If you have affairs you wish to take care of you better be about it."

Mr. Higgins made a partial recovery after his first operation and returned for a time to his ministry in the lumber camp, but it was evident that his condition was serious. He returned to Rochester, Minnesota, for a second operation on October 1, that year (1914).

As his health continued to decline and time for a third operation seemed near, he decided it was time to convene his associates for a last meeting. He was on his way to Chicago to submit to his third and last operation; the one which ended his life. It was a last desperate chance that was offered him by surgery and, characteristically, he took it. He called a meeting of his men in the Duluth YMCA, and to this final historic meeting came Daly, Davis, McCall, Sornberger and Channer.

Frank stood before them and told them of his one chance for recovery, and said he was on his way to the hospital. Then he reviewed the work they had done together, and laid it on their hearts to continue. The leader finished by saying, "Oh, for the days when I could go back into the woods, take the boys by the hand and call them by name: Jim, and John, and Bill. I wish I could turn back the curtain of time and do it all over again. But that I cannot do, and if I have come to the end of the trail *you* will have to do it for me." And he sent those faithful men forth to carry on the Gospel ministry he had begun.

The third operation ended his battle, and the giant fell. He visited Mission Board Headquarters in New York and returned to his boyhood home in Shelburne, Ontario, for a final rest, and there died on January 4, 1915, at the age of 49.

The Board of Home Missions sent a representative to Canada to bring his body back for burial. The funeral service was held at the Town Hall at Delano, Minnesota, and he was laid at rest in neighboring Rockford, in the heart of the country he evangelized for Christ.

Four of his colleagues attended the final rites, together with a great host of ministers and laymen, who came to do honor to a fallen hero. Chief among them was a delegation of unshaven men, dressed in caulked boots and stagged pants, with the callouses of ax-handle, cant-hook, and peavey on their palms. They shed a few tears and they spoke no words, but the lumberjacks were the real and sincere mourners at the funeral of Frank Higgins, the original Sky Pilot.

II
AARON W. MADDOX

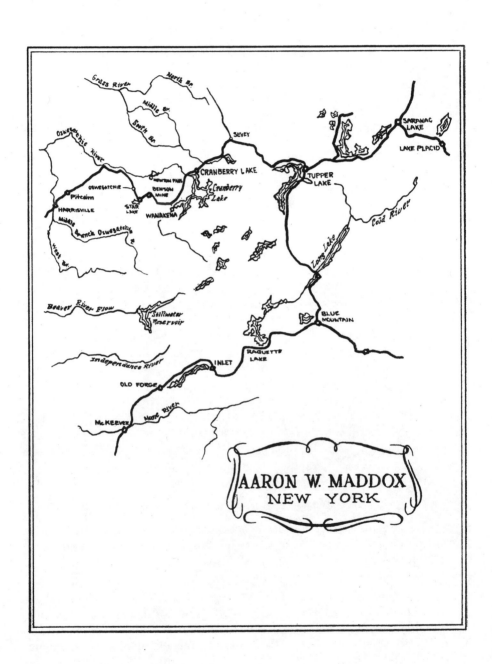

Aaron W. Maddox

Early Life in Brooklyn

Rev. Aaron W. Maddox, who organized the Adirondack Lumber Camp Parish and served as its minister and secretary for twenty-five years, was the key figure in that parish. It was he who saw both the need and the opportunity and went about an organized effort with the helpful assistance of Synodical Superintendent Dr. U. L. Mackey.

Mr. Maddox was born in the city of Brooklyn on November 10, 1873, and attended school in that city. A three-year period at Brooklyn Polytechnic Institute was followed by a year of study at Columbia University, where he graduated in 1896. During college days he decided to enter the ministry and began his preparation at Union Theological Seminary in New York City in the fall of 1896. His graduation from Union Seminary in 1899 was followed by a short term of service as assistant minister in the Lewis Avenue Congregational Church of Brooklyn.

The growing parish duties became somewhat exhausting for the young cleric who decided to visit the doctor. The doctor advised that he had contracted tuberculosis and recommended a prolonged period in the Adirondacks where Doctor Trudeau was helping many to find health through his "rest cure."

The news concerning his serious illness was a shock to Aaron Maddox and members of his family. It meant a delay in or perhaps the end of the career to which he had devoted years of preparation. The illness also meant isolation from many relatives and friends.

Health Failure Leads to the Adirondacks

He and his family decided to take the doctor's advice. He went to Moody on Big Tupper Lake where he took the "rest cure" for the next two years beginning May 12, 1900.

Adirondack air and the "rest cure" brought new strength and vitality within a few months. By the end of two years these remedies had restored him to near normal strength. That led to an important decision. Should he return to the city to resume the ministry which he began with so much promise or should he turn to some other occupation in the mountain country where he had recovered his health? The answer to this

17

question came in the new Presbyterian Church at Tupper Lake Junction where he was asked to serve as Stated Supply and later as pastor. He decided to accept the invitation and took up his duties there in February, 1902. He purchased a small house at Tupper Lake Junction which was to be his home and headquarters for the next half century.

He purchased a lot on the shore of Big Tupper Lake near Moody and built a camp in 1906.

Aaron Maddox was a thorough student, a clear thinker, a man of deep Christian faith, an excellent preacher and a devoted pastor. His Christian character and eloquent preaching soon began to make a profound impression upon the members of the congregation and the people of the growing community.

The effectiveness of his ministry is indicated by the steady growth of the congregation and church membership. He had many opportunities for service to larger churches in New York State cities but decided to continue his ministry in the church at Tupper Lake though the minister's salary was rather small. This was indicative of the reality of his dedication to the service of Christ and his fellowmen.

Tupper Lake was the center of a great lumbering area at that time. Many leaders and workmen in the local forest industries were active in his congregation. Forest industries and logging were the major source of income for his people. He was keenly aware of both their problems and their opportunities. There were several mills in the community at the time.

The "Big Mill" which had been established by John Hurd on the site of the present ball park was operated in the early 1900's by the Norwood Manufacturing Company. Ira B. Hosley and H. H. Day were the partners in this enterprise.

The A. Sherman Lumber Company had a mill on Raquette Pond near to the present site of the Oval Wood Dish Corporation plant.

The Santa Clara Lumber Company operated a sawmill in the lower part of Tupper Lake village and a pulp mill along the Adirondack Division of the New York Central not far from Tupper Lake Junction. They purchased the "Big Mill" from the Norwood Manufacturing Company.

The Brooklyn Cooperage Company operated a mill in the downtown section of Tupper Lake village and had a chemical plant on the present site of the Draper Corporation mill.

The International Paper Company also had a paper mill at Piercefield which was five miles down Raquette River.

These seven mills made Tupper Lake a busy community. They provided employment for most of the people in the community and the income to sustain its economic life.

The softwood logs which made up most of the natural product for the mill activities at the time were driven into the mills on the Raquette River and Big Tupper Lake. The logs of different companies were distinguished by their log marks and were sorted at the big sorting boom on Raquette Pond near the edge of the village. River driving at that time was the major means of transportation for logs and produced an army of highly skilled river drivers who were at home on logs in any kind of water.

The cutting, skidding and transportation of logs to the streams was carried on by another army of old-time lumberjacks some of whom lived in Tupper Lake but many of whom made their homes in the camps and came to town only at Christmas time and at the end of the log haul in mid-March.

The influx of hundreds of old-time lumberjacks into the community at these seasons brought a great boom to business for the clothing stores, shoe stores, hotels, rooming houses and barrooms. The hotels and barrooms came to look upon this as a real harvest season. To them, the lumberjack was a great commercial opportunity and little more. Many of the men who had earned their wages by long hours of hard labor in the woods at all seasons of the year would tell the bartender to set up drinks for the house. After a state of intoxication had overwhelmed the lumberjack he was often relieved of his roll of bills. "Treating the house" and "rolling" soon exhausted his hard earned money. He was then ready for another trip back to hard labor in the forest.

Many of these lumberjacks who had lost their rolls so quickly made their way to the home of Aaron Maddox. Some of them wanted a meal and help for the trip back to camp. Some sought advice and a few came to pray.

Aaron Maddox was greatly disturbed by this condition among the lumberjacks. They were highly skilled and splendid workmen in the woods but had not learned to play. The barrooms took advantage of them on their journeys to town.

The Visit of Frank Higgins

Mr. Maddox learned of the growing ministry of Frank Higgins in the lumber camps of Minnesota. He heard Higgins' address at the meeting of the General Assembly in Atlantic City, New Jersey. He discussed the problem with his good friend, Synodical Superintendent U. L. Mackey.

The two men requested the Board of Home Missions to arrange for a visit by Frank Higgins, who came to Tupper Lake in January, 1913.

Mr. Maddox and Mr. Higgins began with the camps of the Santa Clara Lumber Company on the Cold River which is a branch of the Raquette River. Frank Eldred and Mrs. Eldred, who were employed at Santa Clara headquarters camp, took them to two of the camps with a team and sleigh. Mrs. Eldred, who was a church organist, helped with the singing at the services in the cook camp.

Frank Higgins was a speaker at the church in Tupper Lake on January 20,1913. He had found a friendly spirit and keen interest among the lumberjacks in the Cold River camps as he did later at Woods Lake and in other Adirondack camps.

Higgins' report to a committee from the Synod of New York at a meeting in Utica as he completed his Adirondack camp journey was a vivid and convincing one. Synodical Superintendent U. L. Mackey and his committee moved quickly. At first Aaron Maddox looked for a man of experience in the camps to lead the camp program but found no such person available. Then the committee said to him, "Aaron Maddox, you are the man."

Mr. Maddox offered his resignation to the congregation of the Tupper Lake Church at a meeting on November 16, 1913, in these terms:

"The Synodical Home Missions Committee has elected me as Secretary of Lumber Camp Work. I have accepted this office on condition of your releasing me from the pastorate of this church to be effective January 1, 1914.

"Our work together in this parish has been most pleasant and happy. In all that work, you have given loyal and generous support. For this I thank you and wish to express to you my warmest feelings of love and friendship.

"This has been my only pastorate and I leave it because the Master has called me to work in another part of His vineyard. I ask your prayers for this work as this church shall have mine."

His resignation was accepted by the congregation at its annual meeting on December 14, 1913. On Tuesday evening, March 24, 1914, the friends and parishioners of the Rev. and Mrs. A. W. Maddox tendered them a farewell reception with a large number present.

A major feature of the evening was a musical program by local talent. Attorney Ralph Hastings of Tupper Lake, in a few well-chosen words, outlined the work of Mr. Maddox during the twelve years of his ministry and the lasting impression these labors left upon the community, concluding by the presentation to Mr. Maddox of a purse of gold. Mr. Mad-

Frank Higgins preaching in a lumber camp.
(Photo courtesy Mrs. Wesley Scheer)

A Minnesota logging crew at their log camp.

Frank Higgins hiking on tote road with a heavy pack.

River driving crew at lunch in portable camp.

A crew of old-time lumberjacks at log landing.

Highly skilled river drivers
in white water.

Oval Wood Dish lumber camp at
Kildare (1920).

Sky pilots Aaron Maddox (left)
and Frank Reed (1919).

Frank Eldred of Tupper Lake
took Higgins and Maddox to
camp.

The winter log haul at Newton Falls
(Photo by Newton Falls Paper Company)

dox replied to this in a kindly and feeling manner, pleased to know he was held in such high esteem.

He Becomes a Sky Pilot

As indicated in his resignation, Mr. Maddox began his ministry as sky pilot to Adirondack lumberjacks on January 1, 1914. His first efforts were directed to discovering where the major logging operations were located and who were the key men through whom the ministry in the camps might be introduced. This led to journeys into several areas of the Adirondacks, including such centers as Cranberry Lake, McKeever, Lyons Falls, Poland, Dolgeville, Glens Falls, North Creek, Newcomb and many others. He found keen interest in the program in most of these places.

His visit to Cranberry Lake indicated that worship services in the camps were already an established fact. Charles Atwood was combining a ministry in the church at Cranberry Lake and adjacent communities with a ministry in neighboring lumber camps. W. L. Sykes, who was President of the Emporium Forestry Company, and his family were active churchmen who were keenly interested also in a ministry in the camps. Mr. Atwood was asked to serve on the staff of the new Adirondack Lumber Camp Parish and to combine this work with ministry in the churches. He visited camps around Cranberry Lake and along the Carthage and Adirondack Railroad.

But two men could not meet the needs in the Adirondack lumber camps. There were a large number of camps south of Tupper Lake and many others on Tug Hill and in the eastern and southern Adirondacks. Investigations indicated that there probably were 150 lumber camps in the Adirondacks and that 7,000-8,000 lumberjacks were employed in these camps. Distances involved, the remoteness of some of the camps and the large number of men indicated that a staff of Adirondack sky pilots would be required. Mr. Maddox and Dr. U. L. Mackey continued the search for more men.

Dr. Mackey's efforts were rewarded with a rare find in Rev. C. W. Mason on the occasion of his visit to the parish at Jamesville, New York, which is near to Syracuse. He and Mr. Maddox decided to invite Mr. Mason to become an Adirondack sky pilot. Subsequent events indicated that the hand of the Lord was in the call. C. W. Mason became a well qualified sky pilot and an effective co-worker of Aaron W. Maddox for a quarter of a century.

The Growth of the Lumber Camp Parish

Mr. Maddox and Dr. U. L. Mackey made the following report of the parish in October, 1915.

"This is the second year of the work among the woodsmen of the Adirondacks. A great effort has been made to cover more of the large field, and this has been quite successful. The locations of all but a few camps are now known through personal visits of the missionaries. These visits show that the territory is too large and extended for four men to cover with the desired regularity.

"The parish is in the counties of Clinton, Franklin, St. Lawrence, Lewis, Oneida, Herkimer, Hamilton, Essex and Fulton. On the Hudson River drive there will be work in Warren County, also. A tract of good timber lies in the eastern side of Oswego County, and this may be cut soon. In these counties lumbering is carried on from the camps, and the bunk house life is practically the same in all.

"On the western side lies Tug Hill in Lewis County, the first rise of land east of the Great Lakes. On the eastern side, camps are found nearly to Elizabethtown, one of the beauty spots of the mountains. Southward the parish extends to Salisbury Center, twelve miles north of the Mohawk; and northward camps are located a few miles south of Malone in Franklin County. This is one hundred forty (140) miles north and south, and over one hundred (100) miles east and west.

"There were at least one hundred fifty (150) camps in operation this year. The missionaries visited more than one hundred twenty-five of these. The hope of the mission is to have one man for not more than twenty-five camps, so that frequent visits can be made to each camp.

"As so much soft timber goes now into pulp and much of this is peeled when felled, work has to be started as soon as the bark loosens in May. From then, and until the bark sets in August, large crews are employed. Then the timber is skidded or piled, roads are cut and are made ready for the winter hauling, which is usually finished by the middle of March.

"The river-drives begin as soon as the ice goes out, and there is sufficient water. Some are short, others may last into the summer. This year, and for the first time in the history of lumbering in the Adirondacks, most of the drives were followed by the missionaries. Services were held with the crews, and gospels distributed by our missionaries on 24 drives.

"In the spring, tree planting camps are in operation for a period of from four to eight weeks.. That at Wolf Pond along the D. & H. Railroad in Clinton County had an average of ninety men. This camp was visited, as was that of the Santa Clara Lumber Company near Ampersand Pond in Franklin County. There will be more of this work, because tree planting must be done both by the State and private holders, if the North Woods are to continue as a source of timber. Thousands of acres, now denuded, can be made to yield a valuable crop of timber, and the growth of trees will materially increase the water supply for manufacturing purposes. They will, at the same time, add greatly to the beauty of the country. Highways are being built and improved and, in the labor camps which follow them, the missionary can distribute gospels and occasionally hold service. The same is true of construction camps on logging railroads. Most of the men in such camps are Italians, but Spaniards and Mexicans are met with, and some Irish, French Canadians, and Americans.

"Services were held in several settlements, among them being Mc-Keever, Otter Lake, Onchiota, Rainbow Sanitorium (of the Independent Order of Foresters), Brandreth Lake, Brandreth Station, Childwold, Axton and Morehouseville.

"The parishioners met in this work are nearly all men. In some camps women do the cooking, and here and there families are found. The foremen will sometimes bring in their wives and children. The tone of the camps is better for the presence of women, and some of these women stay in the woods for weeks at a time. To do the cooking for twenty to fifty men, especially during the log hauling, when breakfast is served at four o'clock in the morning and the last teamster is often not in until seven at night, is no easy job. Yet many of these women are most efficient, and it is the testimony of all the missionaries that their cooking is never excelled by the men.

"The woodsmen are of many nationalities: Irish, English, American, Spanish, Norwegian, Swedish, French Canadian, American Indian, Lithuanian, Polish, Russian, Italian, German and Roumanian.

"Gospels furnished to the extent of one hundred dollars' worth by the American Bible Society, and coming also from other friends of the work, have been given out in ten languages: English, French, Spanish, Italian, Lithuanian, Swedish, Polish, Russian, Roumanian and German. Hungarian Bibles have also been requested.

"The woodsmen are of all sorts and conditions, all degrees of moral development and intelligence, and of several religions or none at all. One foreman, in giving permission for a service, said he did not think religion troubled his men much. But not infrequently men are seen to kneel and say their prayers before getting into their bunks at night, and some of those who go out to a village over Sunday attend church. This, however, is far from being the practice. The camp service is the only religious service many of them ever see, and a sermon to them is a desirable novelty.

"Members of the parish staff are:

"(1) Rev. Aaron W. Maddox of Faust has continued as secretary of the work, and has been actively engaged in directing the mission. He has

23

made a large survey, and has been over, now, most of the Adirondacks. Besides preaching in the camps he has found it advisable to give some attention to small settlements without settled pastors, and in this has helped as he could the Presbyterial Missions operating in the Adirondacks. He has been called upon to preach in various churches, celebrate the communion, and moderate a vacant session. As interest in the work has increased, he with some of the other field workers has presented the cause in a number of churches both of our own and other denominations.

"(2) Rev. Charles Atwood of Oswegatchie covers a territory of fifty miles square, and visits about twenty-five camps. He preaches in five of the stations of the Adirondack Mission of St. Lawrence Presbytery also, and is a man of devotion and force for good in his large field.

"(3) Mr. Edwin K. Coughran, of Akron, N.Y., went to the McKeever district in November, and stayed until the middle of June, when he left to continue his college course at Cornell University. Besides preaching in the camps and at McKeever, he looked after the neglected Pinney Settlement, and made that a Home Department of his Sunday School at McKeever.

"(4) Rev. C. W. Mason was called to the work from his pastorate of the Jamesville, N.Y., Presbyterian Church in February, and gave his entire time to the camps. He was very sick in May and June, but is fully recovered. As his trips are long, and he is out several weeks at a time, he uses a burro to pack his duffle. Mr. Mason is an experienced woodsman.

"(5) Mr. Melville G. Montgomery, a student in Union Theological Seminary, took Mr. Coughran's place in June, and was in the field during the summer. Services were continued at McKeever and several small settlements, and arrangments were made by him for regular preaching during the summer in Pinney Settlement. In addition to this a number of ministers have been in the region during the year, and have loaned their services as opportunity was given.

"Quantities of magazines have been sent in to the camps, names being furnished by the workers; 'First Aid' has been given, and even money furnished to men in need. For all of these kinds of service there is a large field.

"Events of interest:

"(1) The Secretary and Mr. Mason took part in a campaign for No-License in the town of Waverly, Franklin County, in March. The temperance forces won at both the regular Town Meeting and at a special election ordered by the court. The Mission is decidedly against liquor traffic.

"(2) A missionary had given a young Italian a gospel and the next

24

day as he was walking along the state road to a lumber camp, the Italian met him, and proudly holding up the Gospel said, 'Me hava him.'

"(3) The sermons are full of the name of Jesus Christ, and he is referred to constantly. Ah! but the name of the Master is heard all too frequently used by the men in cursing and profanity.

"(4) As Dr. Grenfell practiced medicine for the Glory of God, these men are told they can roll logs, drive team, make roads, and do the work of the woods for His praise and glory. Religion is preached as something for every day.

"With two more field workers the entire parish could be well covered. There should be at a central place like Tupper Lake Junction, a Woodsmen's Building on the plan of the Industrial Y.M.C.A. Such a building would have a small hospital, dormitories, restaurant, baths and reading rooms, and would be in charge of a trained secretary. Mr. Maddox will be glad to furnish information."

Frank Reed came to join the staff of the Adirondack Lumber Camp Parish in April, 1917, with headquarters at McKeever. He left at the end of a year to serve with the American Expeditionary Forces in France and returned to the lumber camps in the late winter of 1919. He was destined to spend a half century in the North Woods with much of that service in the lumber camps.

The Growing Influence of Aaron Maddox

Aaron Maddox continued his active supervision of the lumber camp parish program for many years. He took many trips to lumber camps in company with other sky pilots including Charles Atwood, Clarence Mason, Jack Logan and Frank Reed. Production levels continued high in forest products for some years after World War I and several men were needed to carry on the camp visitation program.

Mr. Maddox was called on to tell the story of the lumber camps in many churches, schools and service clubs over an increasing radius. He also had a keen interest in the small churches and rural communities in Northern New York where it was difficult to maintain year round operations and a vigorous ministry.

With the coming of the Big Depression in 1929 the demand for forest products declined. By the winter of 1932-1933, the number of lumber camps in the Adirondacks had declined from 150 to about 20. Many men were unemployed. Clarence Mason was able to carry the complete load of camp visitation throughout the Adirondacks.

Mr. Maddox turned his attention during that period more to the small churches and rural communities which were having increasing

25

difficulties in maintaining a vigorous and fruitful program. He conducted Sunday worship services in the churches, communion services, funeral services, weddings and baptisms. His record book lists 502 baptisms in a wide variety of communities including Childwold, Cranberry Lake, Star Lake, Russell, Paul Smith's, Santa Clara, Onchiota, Tupper Lake and other places. The number of weddings and funerals is also numerous, indicating the esteem in which he was held.

The talents and Christian spirit of Mr. Maddox were viewed with increasing appreciation by a widening circle of friends and admirers. He was elected as Moderator of the Synod of New York and served with distinction for a year in that capacity. At the peak of his career, he was undoubtedly the best known and most highly respected man in Northern New York.

With the retirement of Clarence Mason and the return of Frank Reed to full time service in the camps in 1938, Aaron Maddox retired from active participation in the lumber camp program and gave his full time to the ministry of the small churches and rural communities where he continued to exert a profound influence until his death in 1952.

Mr. Maddox passed away in Bermuda on March 12, 1952. The funeral service was conducted by Rev. Alvin Gurley of Saranac at the church in Tupper Lake where he had begun his long and fruitful ministry and which he left in 1913 to become the pioneer sky pilot in the Adirondack lumber camps.

The memory of him will linger long in the minds of those who knew him over a very wide area. His influence will live long in the character of many other younger people whose lives have been enriched by the eloquence of his preaching, the sincerity of his purpose, the depth of his love and the reality of his dedication.

III

CHARLES ATWOOD

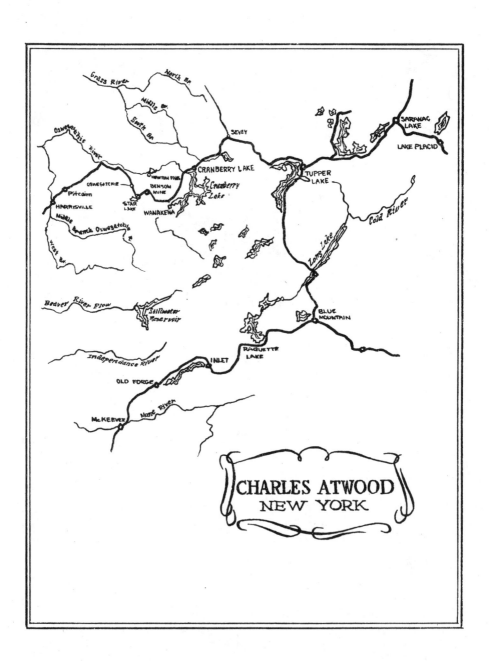

CHARLES ATWOOD
NEW YORK

Charles Atwood

Early Life in England

Charles Atwood was born in Staffordshire, England, on March 4, 1860, but spent most of his life in the Adirondack Mountains. His parents joined the army of people who were coming to America after the Civil War and settled at Fulton, New York, where Mr. Atwood set up a chain shop which he operated for many years.

Charles divided his time between work in the chain shop, where he acquired real skill, and his studies at Falley Seminary, in which he was an industrious and successful student.

The influence of a Christian home, the local church and Falley Seminary were vital factors in his decision to enter the Christian ministry. Following his graduation from Falley Seminary, he became the supply pastor at a mission church which was supported by the First Presbyterian Church of Fulton. He also gave part time service in his father's chain shop.

Charles married Hattie Covill of Fulton in 1882. She shared with him in a fruitful ministry at Fulton and in the Adirondacks.

A breakdown in health in 1900 caused the young minister to seek medical advice concerning his future plans. The doctors advised an extended period of rest and treatment in the Adirondacks. He decided to take the physician's advice and went to Cranberry Lake in 1901 in search of better health.

The rest and quiet of the Cranberry Lake area had the desired result. After a few months, Mr. Atwood returned to his parish in Fulton for four years of devoted service.

Call to Oswegatchie Parish

The memory of the months in the Cranberry Lake section lingered long with him, however, and he decided to cast his lot with the people of the North Country. He went to Oswegatchie, New York, where he accepted the pastorate of a small church in the village and made that church the center of a far-flung parish for the next seven years. The new parish included pioneer work in the communities of Benson Mines, Newbridge, Newton Falls, Star Lake, and Wanakena, along with Oswegatchie.

29

A very significant development of the new parish centering at Oswegatchie was the opportunity for a Christian ministry in neighboring lumber camps which were numerous at that time in the area.

Lloyd Bassette was operating some camps south of Star Lake and at Streeter Lake where he was cutting pulpwood for Ball Brothers of Carthage. William Sayers was the logging superintendent for Ball Brothers, who were pulp and paper manufacturers, but Mr. Bassette was the pulpwood contractor.

John Kerr had logging operations for the Middle River Lumber Company, who had a sawmill in the village of Aldrich.

Clarence Strife ran the sawmill for some time. Jerome Farrell was president of the company in 1917 with Peter Yousey as a jobber.

The Newton Falls Paper Company also had a 7,000-acre tract in the area and built the railroad from Aldrich to Streeter Lake.

Post and Henderson had a sawmill and logging operations near the Herkimer County line south of Star Lake. Their mill and camps were served by a railroad spur running out from Benson Mines.

R. W. Higbie purchased a 21,500-acre tract in the town of Clifton in 1905 and built a railroad from Newton Falls to Newbridge where he established a large mill. This mill operated until 1915.

The Webster Lumber Company operated a mill on the Oswegatchie River at Hardwood Mill in the early 1900's.

Lumbering at Wanakena

The Rich and Andrews Lumber Company purchased a large tract of forest land in 1901 in the Wanakena area where they developed extensive logging operations and an integrated milling program. The company established the village of Wanakena where they located their office and company store. They constructed a system of railroads for the transportation of logs and the manufactured products. Giddeon Wilson was superintendent of company operations.

Most of the manufacturing in this multi-product program was done on a contract basis. Ford Brothers operated a large mill to saw the softwood into lumber. The mill had a large pond for storage of the logs on the way to the sawmill. Henry Venters had a heading mill to manufacture barrel heads from hardwood. These were sold to cooperage manufacturers. Charles Bates operated a shoe last factory and Mr. Northrup a whip butt mill. The latter made butts for whips used in buggies and wagons. Rhine and Slayter operated a plant to chip slabs for use in the paper mills.

The area around Wanakena and Cranberry Lake had a large number of lumber camps to supply the mills at Wanakena with logs and the Newton Falls paper mill with necessary pulpwood. The pulpwood was boomed on Cranberry Lake and driven down the Oswegatchie to the paper mill. Most of the logs for the Wanakena mills were transported by rail.

The list of logging and pulpwood operators in the area at the time included Duncan MacDonald, George MacDonald, T. Dumoulin, the John MacDonald Lumber Company, Clark and Squires, and Warren Guinip.

The new minister-sky pilot led a busy life during these active logging days. He conducted religious services on Sunday at the church in Oswegatchie but spent most of the week in the other villages and neighboring lumber camps where he was well received by the hundreds of old-time lumberjacks.

Company executives at the mills and on the Carthage and Adirondack railroad were in sympathy with Mr. Atwood's parish program. They gave him permission to use a speeder on the railroad as an improved method of transportation in his large parish. The speeder was equipped with special wheels and was propelled by foot power like a bicycle. With this improved method of transportation, he was able to reach the outlying villages and many of the camps over the railroad tracks.

Mr. Atwood was fond of the woods as well as the men in his vast parish. His favorite sport was fishing and he found time for occasional fishing trips to provide relaxation from his arduous labors. Mr. William Griffin of Star Lake recently told the writer of several fishing trips which he took with Mr. Atwood when he was a small boy.

In the year 1911 two significant events took place which profoundly affected Mr. Atwood's program.

The supply of timber to operate the mills around Oswegatchie and Wanakena was nearing the point of exhaustion for current operations. The Rich and Andrews Lumber Company brought their operations to a close in 1912. This meant that there were few lumber camps and old-time lumberjacks in the immediate area.

The Emporium Forestry Company of Galeton, Pennsylvania, opened a new mill at Conifer, New York, in 1911 and, soon after, completed the Grasse River railroad to Cranberry Lake. This brought about a shift in lumber operations and camps from Wanakena to the Cranberry Lake and Conifer areas. Many of Mr. Atwood's parishioners moved to the new locations.

Move to Cranberry Lake

Mr. Atwood made the logical move. He resigned as minister of the church at Oswegatchie and moved to Cranberry Lake where he served part-time as minister of the church while he continued his work as sky pilot to the lumberjacks.

As time went on and the World War I period approached, the tempo of logging in the Conifer-Cranberry Lake area increased. The Emporium Forestry Company increased their activities under the leadership of the President, W. L. Sykes. More railroads were constructed to areas of operation such as Newbridge and Claire where rail transportation opened up virgin forest areas, and a new mill was built at Cranberry Lake in 1917.

Several camps were also in operation around Cranberry Lake where the lake could be used for the transportation of supplies as well as logs. Softwood logs were handled in booms on Cranberry Lake by a large steamboat. The hardwood logs around the lake were transported on softwood racks which were also towed by the steamboat.

The list of active operators for the Emporium Forestry Company at the time included: John Davignon, Ovid DeCoss, Jesse Lyons, Fred Moore, Sam Laboard, George Bushey and Oliver Proulx.

Mr. Atwood went to one of the lumber camps on a very cold night when the temperature was more than 40 below zero. The stove wood was wet and green so the fire was not as good as usual. "My lad," said the boss, "If you preach hell fire here tonight, you will miss it. Every man here would like a little of the warm place." Mr. Atwood preached the warmth of Heaven and won the men.

Shortly after his assignment to the Adirondack Lumber Camp Parish in January, 1914, Aaron Maddox visited Cranberry Lake and spent some time with Charles Atwood, as well as the Emporium Forestry Company. He invited Mr. Atwood to join the staff of the parish on a part-time basis along with his responsibilities in the church at Cranberry Lake. Mr. Atwood decided to accept the invitation to share with other men in a ministry to Adirondack lumberjacks, a ministry which he had already carried on by himself for some years.

Charles Atwood continued to serve the church at Cranberry Lake and his vast lumber camp parish vigorously for the next seven years until 1921 when he resigned as minister of the church in order to devote full time to his work in the lumber camps.

(The writer shared with Mr. Atwood in his last service at the Cranberry Lake Church in the summer of 1921 and later introduced him in several camps along the Adirondack Division of the New York Central south of Tupper Lake.)

Mr. Atwood continued his work as sky pilot to Adirondack lumberjacks over a somewhat wider area for the next seven years until a stroke in January, 1928, brought an end to his active ministry.

His Illness and Death

He then spent some time with Mrs. Atwood at the homes of their daughters: Mrs. Arthur Jones of Bradford, Pennsylvania, and Mrs. John Storm of Fulton, New York. Mrs. Atwood died in 1934.

Charles Atwood passed away at the home of his daughter, Mrs. Arthur Jones, in Bradford, in 1937 and was laid at rest in Mount Adnah Cemetery in Fulton, New York. In addition to Mrs. Jones and Mrs. Storm, he is survived by a son, Charles, who is International President of Union Carbide and Chemical Company.

Charles Atwood was a man of boundless energy, sterling character and great dedication, who contributed much to the lives of both community residents and Adirondack lumberjacks. His ministry will continue to stand as one of the remarkable events of Adirondack history.

IV

CLARENCE W. MASON

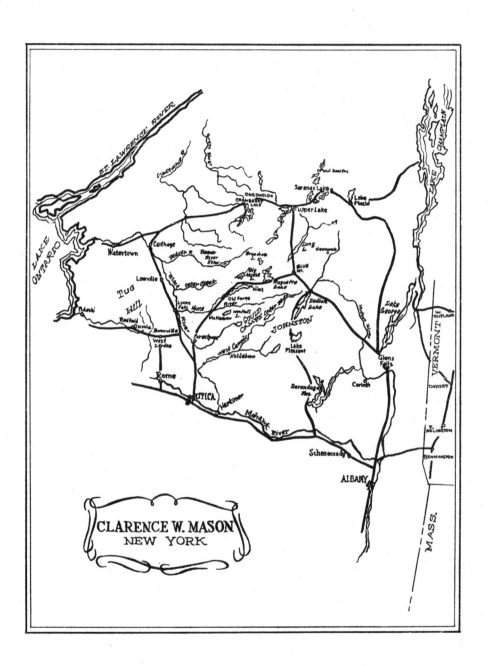

CLARENCE W. MASON
NEW YORK

36

Clarence W. Mason

Early Life in Central New York

Clarence W. Mason was born on a farm near Vernon Center in Oneida County, New York, on March 11, 1868, but his journeys took him far from that community into the heart of the Adirondack wilderness in places where few men travelled.

His early life included studies in the one-room district school up the Big Hill on the way to Clinton and varied duties on the farm where he became familiar with plowing and planting, the cultivation of crops, haying and harvesting, and other farm activities. Harvesting was done then with the cradle which he learned to use with proficiency. Farm transportation at the time was furnished largely by the ox which he learned to break and drive as a part of daily life on the farm.

Clarence took his high school training at Best's Boys School in Clinton where he was an excellent student. When he completed his high school work, he entered Hamilton College at Clinton but continued to live on the home farm, where he helped with the farm chores before taking up his studies in the evening. The six-mile journey on foot to and from college laid a suitable foundation for his later and longer journeys to Adirondack lumber camps. He was also an active member of Hamilton College's first football team.

Upon graduation from Hamilton College, Mr. Mason decided upon the Christian ministry as a profession and enrolled for the first two years at Union Theological Seminary in New York City. He transferred to McCormick Theological Seminary in Chicago for his last year of training.

The people of neighboring Deansboro knew of his Christian sincerity and his achievements in college and seminary. The Congregational Church there called him to be its pastor following his Seminary graduation in 1895. He married Gertrude Nanktelow of Westmoreland in 1899 and brought her back to the manse in Deansboro.

He was called to the Congregational Church at Port Leyden, New York, in 1904. There he became a close friend of Dr. Frank Bigarel and was well acquainted with his neighbor, Dr. William H. Johnston, the father of John E. Johnston.

His experience on the farm was a valuable asset to his ministry at the churches in Deansboro, Port Leyden and Jamesville. The farmers in his congregation found that he could pitch hay or milk a cow and was willing to help out in an emergency.

In later years, he and Dr. Bigarel built a hunting camp at Garrett Lake in the Adirondack foothills, which he made the center of his hunting activities for many years.

In 1909 he was called to be the pastor of the Presbyterian Church in Jamesville, where he had an active pastorate and was also effective in helping young men who had been sentenced to Onondaga County Penitentiary.

An Adirondack Sky Pilot

In 1914, when Synodical Superintendent Dr. U. L. Mackey was seeking men for the Adirondack Lumber Camp Parish, he spent a week-end with Mr. Mason at Jamesville. The visit convinced him that there was the man who was needed in the Adirondack lumber camps. He passed the suggestion on to Rev. Aaron W. Maddox at Tupper Lake who, like Dr. Mackey, agreed that Mr. Mason was a man of rare experience for the ministry in the lumber camps. He was called to the Adirondack Lumber Camp Parish in 1915.

The education of four daughters was a major problem confronting Mr. and Mrs. Mason. In 1918 they decided to move to Ithaca where the girls could live at home and study at Cornell University. Mrs. Mason rented rooms to Cornell students to help meet college expenses.

Mr. Mason thus described his first visit in an early issue of *The Lumber Camp News.*

"It is 24 years since I had my first service in a lumber camp. That was in the camp of Pete Gumlaw and he was jobbing for the Rogers Company of Ausable Forks. His camp was on the west branch of the Ausable River, not far from Lake Placid.

"It is a far cry and many a long mile from that camp on the Ausable where I had my first service, until I had my last one in March, 1938.

"That was up past Number Four on the Beaver River Flow and it was a camp of the Little Rapids Lumber Company. Frank Dakir, of Croghan was foreman and Louis Holland and his wife, Minnie, were the shanty keepers. They were good cooks, as were likewise Louis' brother, Fred Holland, and his wife Ada. They cooked for a good many years in camps for Jim Canan when he was lumbering for the Gould Paper Co.

"I drove the car within ten minutes walk from that last camp. It was

38

a wet afternoon and the men came in that night pretty badly soaked with the melting snow and rains. I was somewhat concerned about the roads, as we were far back in the woods and we had to cross quite an extensive swamp. But they had been hauling wood out on trucks all winter and the roads were solid ice. Besides it turned colder during the night and there was no trouble about getting out.

"I shall not forget that last service. I can shut my eyes yet and see it all so plainly. I bid the men goodbye regretfully, knowing I might not ever be in a lumber camp again."

Mr. Mason's annual program in the Adirondack lumber camps consisted of spending the busy peeling, skidding and hauling season in the camps and then a short time with his family in Ithaca during the slack periods between seasons such as Christmas time and late March. He also made many of the river drives in the spring.

At first Mr. Mason traveled on foot, carrying a knapsack; or in winter on snowshoes dragging a toboggan-like sled. His snowshoes were six feet long and very narrow to avoid snagging in the brush. He later acquired a burro named Texas but her braying was a problem. Next came a black mare named Bess who knew the woods and could walk a corduroy road, as sure-footed as a cat, pulling a buckboard.

Finally the machine age arrived and he began driving a car. The first of these was a model T Ford which came knocked down. He and Oscar Hines of Jamesville, who was a born mechanic, put it together. He drove this Ford far enough to encircle the earth ten times. Mr. Mason replaced the Ford with a Dodge touring car and the Dodge with a Plymouth sedan which he, at first, considered rather sissy. He did admit that the sedan was more comfortable in winter. By that time, there were many more improved roads in the Adirondacks and some of them were kept open in winter.

During his early years in the camps, he would open his activities of the hauling season by coming to the Adirondacks right after Christmas. He might start his trip around Lake Placid as he did on his first journey and work southward through the woods from one logging operation and camp to another. Many of these trips were made through the woods where there were no roads. Adirondack highways were not plowed in winter at that time so he used the snowshoes for most of his winter travels. The condition of the snow surface determined his rate of travel. For instance, his sixteen-mile journey from Lake Cora to the Cedar Lakes took three days after a deep fall of fresh snow. He made the same trip on hard snow the following year in nine hours.

A Narrow Escape on Ice

Mr. Mason thus relates the story of some of these journeys. "One of the strangest experiences I ever had while traveling in the woods was while Pat Wallace was running a job for the International Paper Company on Jessup River. It was mid-winter during the log haul, and on a morning when the thermometer registered way down below zero. At that time The Union Bag Company was lumbering in the West Canada Lakes. I planned to cross the woods on snowshoes from the camp on the Jessup River to the West Canada.

"A flood dam had been built in the outlet of Moose pond, a mile or more above Wallace's camp, and the planks were all in to keep the flow ground full for the log drive in the spring. When I reached the flow ground, I left the main haul along the Jessup River, and started across the flow intending to keep on the ice until I reached the far side of Moose Pond.

"It was such a cold morning, I don't know why it was I became suspicious of the ice, but I did; and determined to get on the shore of the flow, skirt along the edge of it, and take to the ice again across Moose Pond. Acting on this plan. I started toward the shore. I walked on the ice up to a spruce tree that had fallen from its place near the edge of the flow and reached far out from the shore, I stepped onto the trunk of the tree and stood there a moment. There was still quite a distance between me and the shore. Apparently there was solid ice ahead, covered with a blanket of snow.

"I started to step off the tree out onto the ice, and go ashore. But my snowshoes went right down into open water; and I went into the water with them. I went feet first, and that is also strange, for one naturally leans forward when about to take a step forward. It is a wonder that I didn't plunge off head first, and if I had, encumbered as I was with my snowshoes, I should probably have drowned. I shall never know how deep the water was; but I have always figured it was at least eight feet deep. I went down into it half my length, which was three feet and the snowshoes two feet farther made five feet, and no sign of touching bottom. Well, my elbows caught on the tree trunk, and that saved me from going down any farther into the water.

"I dragged myself back up onto the tree trunk and untied the leather thongs which held the snowshoes on my feet. I shoved the snowshoes back a little, and stood up on the tree trunk. And then I saw what seemed to me the strangest part of it all. My snowshoes lay in open water back of me. I made up my mind I had better stay on the tree, so I worked my way through the branches, and reached the shore.

"My wet clothes promptly froze stiff as a stove pipe. As soon as I could get out of the wind, I took off my shoes and wrung the water out of my socks, put them on again and traveled along. When I reachd Mud Lake, I could see the team hauling the water box down the main haul on the north side of Mud Lake. Frank Husson and Louis Ovitt were watering the road. I crossed the lake, and walked up the road to the camp. When the team came back with the water box, Frank said to Louis, 'Mr. Mason is up at camp.' 'How do you know?' Louis answered, 'Why, there is his snowshoe track. No one else has a pair of snowshoes like that.' (They were my six-foot Peary shoes.)

"Tim Buckley was chore boy at camp. When I walked in Tim said, 'You look as if you had been in water.' " 'Yes, Tim, I have been, I got into Moose flow'."

" 'Well, well, now. We'll have to see about that.'

"So he put a lot of kindling and kerosene into the big box stove, and soon had both stove and pipe red-hot. I stood up by the stove and turned around and around, like a goose roasting on a spit. My clothes were very quickly dried out."

*   *   *   *   *   *   *

Caught in a Snow Slide

"When John Beebe was lumbering at Elk Lake, I visited his camp during the log haul. The snow was very deep in the mountains that winter. At some time during my stay at the camp I said that I intended to go through St. Hubert's Pass and visit the Rogers Camps on the East branch of the Ausable River.

"Paddy Heffron was working at the Beebe camp at the time. (He was an ex-sailor and he picked up quite a bit of money from the sale of models of full-rigged sailing ships he made.) Paddy came and sat beside me and leaning over, said in a whisper, 'Did I hear you say that you planned to go through St. Hubert's Pass?' I told him that was my intention.

" 'Well,' he said, 'I wouldn't do it; you had better go around by the road.' It would have been at least 50 miles by road and it was only ten or twelve miles through the pass. I consider St. Hubert's Pass steeper and rougher than the Indian or Avalanche Pass and I have been through all of them a number of times both in summer and in winter.

"I started from the Beebe camp sometime during the afternoon, taking along a lunch which I ate at the old set of Hunter Camps which I passed on my way.

"It was a steep and laborious climb to the summit of the pass and it was well on in the afternoon when I was ready to start down the long descent on the north side. The snow at the summit was at least eight feet deep. There had been a sleet storm and the snow was covered with a hard, smooth crust. After the sleet storm there had been more snowfall, and now a depth of about two feet of new snow lay there on the crust.

"At the summit there was quite a field, nearly level, comparatively smooth, and with only here and there a stunted tree. I crossed this open space and was thinking, 'Now I am up at the top and I shall have a downhill haul clear into St. Hubert's.' I didn't know there was a smooth crust down about two feet under the surface of the snow or I might have been a little more cautious.

"Soon I came to a place where the surface inclined downward quite sharply and a whole field of the snow with me in about the center of it, began to slide. A balsam tree about five inches in diameter stood almost in front of me. I put my hand against it thinking that it would stop me but it went over as if nothing had been there.

"We kept on going, a little faster all the time as the incline steepened, until we finally came to a stop at the bottom of a narrow, rocky gorge. I wasn't completely buried in the snow, but nearly so.

"You have no idea how hard the snow was packed. It took me a little while to dig myself out. My long snowshoes were in there, completely buried, and they were well tied onto my feet. I had no shovel with me. Neither the camp axe nor my knife served very well in such a situation.

"It was nearly dark when I finally worked myself free, and there was no place at hand to pass the night. I picked my way down that steep, rocky gorge for perhaps a quarter of a mile and came to a place where there was a little firewood for the night, and plenty of browse to mark a good shakedown on the snow mattress. In fact the night at Big Slide Mountain was the only time I ever camped out in the snow with a good supply of browse.

"The stars sparkled brightly in the roof of my bed chamber, and the next forenoon when I reached Duquette's house at St. Hubert's the thermometer registered 10 degrees below zero."

*　*　*　*　*　*　*

A Winter Night at Big Slide Mountain

"One February afternoon at about 2 o'clock I left South Meadows on my way to visit a Rogers camp near Keene Valley. The snow that day was soft and crumbly; a little too deep to get along without snow-

42

shoes, and not deep enough nor solid enough to make good walking with them. My course led past the foot of Big Slide Mountain.

"That section had been lumbered years before. The old skid bridges on the logging roads had rotted and broken down in many places. Forest fires had swept over the area, burning up the old slash and almost everything except the rocks. And after the fire, the whole section had been covered with a thick growth of pin cherries.

"Altogether it made slow traveling and by the time I reached the height of ground, it was nearly night. It was still several miles down to Keene Valley. I couldn't possibly reach there until long after dark.

"The area having been burned over, there wasn't a bit of green timber to be found. What I mean is that there wasn't anything with which to make a browse bed—no spruce, balsam, cedar or hemlock. I kept going a good while after I knew I ought to stop, in hopes that I would find a few trees with browse.

"That country from several miles away looks as smooth as a lawn, but when in the midst of it, one finds it very rough with many big boulders and abrupt precipitous ledges. I was afraid that I might fall in some rough spot and have a bad accident. I finally stopped in the midst of a thicket of pin cherry. There was a big boulder there and a dead softwood tree lay over a hummock, its top sticking out into the air at a convenient height and covered with resinous knots, hard and dry as matches.

"It took but a few minutes to knock some of them off, split them into kindling wood, whittle some shavings and start a fire. The firewood that night for the most part was pin cherry. It made a good hot fire, only it had to be replenished oftener than if it had been larger wood. I put up my sheltercloth roof, spread out my waterproof knapsack to its fullest extent, and slept on that a good part of the night.

"In February, the first streaks of dawn appear about 6:30. I stirred up my fire, resorted to my sack of emergency rations, made my breakfast from that, packed up my kit and started again toward Keene Valley.

"When I reached Interbrook Lodge on the John Brook trail, I found some men with a team and sleigh filling the ice house for the summer guests. As I was walking along, the man on the load of ice called to me and asked, 'Hey there, where did you come from?' "I said, 'I came from South Meadows.'

" 'Well, when did you start from there?'

" 'About 2 o'clock yesterday afternoon.'

" 'But where did you stay last night?'

" 'In a camp at the foot of Big Slide Mountain.'

" 'There ain't any camp there.'

43

" 'Well, there was last night; I made one.'

" 'Hey, Bill,' he called to the man inside the ice house, 'this guy out here says he camped out last night at the foot of Big Slide Mountain. Did you ever hear the like of that?' "

*   *   *   *   *   *   *

Escape from a Falling Rock

"Once while crossing the woods on snowshoes from the old Gould Camp No. 6 on the Indian River, of which Gardner Poor was foreman, to the Raquette Lake country, I had a peculiar experience. I was out three nights in the woods and this happened the last night of the three.

"As it was getting late in the afternoon of the third day, I began to look for a favorable place to pass the night. I soon saw a large object, some distance away, which looked like a building, and I thought perhaps it might be an old camp building. When I reached it, I found it was huge rock, as large as a fair-sized house.

"On one side, an overhang slanted far back like an open shed roof and down under it there was no snow and I could see dry grass and leaves. I thought, 'Well here is a good camping place all ready prepared.' It wasn't long before I had a hot fire burning before this open shed-like place. I was busy getting more wood for the night and some browse for my bed when I noticed a good deal of water had begun to drip from what might be called eaves of the shed. It threatened not only to put out the fire, but to flood the entire lower floor of the house. You see there was about four feet of snow on the roof and the heat of the fire began to melt it. I could see at once that my plan to use that place as a bed chamber was a mistake.

"Around the corner was a sheer perpendicular wall of rock and I determined to move around there and establish my camp where I wouldn't be in so much need of an umbrella. With a snowshoe I shoveled out a trench and transferred the fire and camp duffle from the west to the north bedroom.

"As I was digging out the trench along the face of the rock, I noticed a dark perpendicular seam running from the top to the bottom and about four feet from the corner. Around the corner and about four feet from the corner was another dark seam running from the top to the bottom of the rock. I thought, 'Now wouldn't it be possible, since I have had a good fire on one side, that when the fire gets the rock warm on the other side, that whole corner of the rock might loosen and fall over.' Anyway I decided the thing to do would be to keep away from it.

"While getting more night wood, by the light of the camp fire, I glanced over my shoulder just in time to see that whole corner of the rock

44

split off and fall over into the snow with a great 'phluff.' If I had been under it when it fell, I might have been there yet, unless 'Mossy' Maxam had found me as he ranged through that section of the woods, hunting and trapping. That big section of the rock must have weighed well over a ton.

"That is not quite the whole story or the most peculiar part of it, though it was the most dangerous part. Something else happened by that rock I never had happen before or since.

"By being obliged to change the location of my camp and start all over again, it was quite late when I was finally ready to lie down and go to sleep on my bed of browse, before the fire. I had had a long tramp on snowshoes and I slept soundly, waking up as I usually did about every two hours to replenish the fire. The last time I awoke it was growing light and it felt very cold. I bestirred myself to get some dry wood on the fire, when I found, to my astonishment, that the fire had completely disappeared. Unknown to me, since I had built the fire as I always did in the winter, right on the surface of the snow, there were fissures in the rock under the fire and when the sticks of firewood had burned down to coals they had disintegrated and had dropped way down out of sight in those cracks in the rock. I must have overslept on that last heat or I should have waked up in time to keep the fire going."

* * * * * * *

The sky pilot also relates stories of near accidents and spectacular escapes on the log haul.

Horse Has a Miraculous Escape

"Ernie Brooks had a camp one year at Whittaker Lake, five or six miles from Speculator. Part of the job was across the lake, on and around Dug Mountain; I think he was jobbing for the International Paper Company. I never knew why he did it, but he built double headers quite a distance up the side of Dug Mountain. I suppose he had a good reason for starting his main haul from there. Both Ernie and Ed Brooks were good lumbermen; they were brought up in the woods; their father was a lumberman before them. Soon after the loads left the double headers, they went down quite a steep hill, then across a short piece of road that was nearly level, and then down another hill, a little longer and just as steep, and at the foot of the second hill, there was a sharp turn to the right.

"One morning during the log haul, it was snowing quite fast and someone at the camp remarked that if the boys didn't watch out, someone would be taking a ride down the mountain. What they meant was

45

that the snow coming so fast would cover the guarding on the hills and someone might get sluiced. About ten o'clock in the forenoon we heard some men shouting up near where they were loading the logs, and sure enough the expected had happened. A man they called 'Clocky' Cole was driving a young team, Cub and Bony. Clocky tried desperately hard to stop the load, but the load was so heavy and was under such headway that before the teams could stop it they went over the brow of the next hill. Then, in spite of all they could do, the load began to go faster again, and to save themselves the team made a run for it. They were young and quick on their feet and were just turning the corner into the straight. I believe they would have made it all right, but just at that critical time the bail chain and the bellyband on Cub's side broke.

"It let everything loose—Clocky rolled off the top of the load into the snow—Bony swung wide out of the track; the load swept by him and stripped all the harness from him except the collar. But Cub and the load went over into the boulder-strewn bed of the stream which was on his side of the road. The horse fell among some large boulders and the load piled over him. He was completely buried under the logs—you wouldn't have known there was a horse there.

A gang of men with peavies rolled and pried the logs off one by one and finally got down to the horse. A long wrapping chain was brought and tied to the collar. A dozen or fifteen of us gave a big pull on the chain and the horse came up onto his feet. He shook the snow off and picked his way carefully along, up into the road. They took him down to the barn and put his blanket on him. There didn't appear to be anything wrong with him, and in a day or two he and his mate were hauling logs again.

Clocky had picked himself up out of the snow. He was not hurt, but he turned his back and walked away. He didn't want to look, for he thought certainly one of his fine teams had been killed, and no wonder he thought so, under the circumstances. But strange enough, Cub came out of the scrape without a scratch."

*　*　*　*　*　*　*

Team Sluiced on a Steep Mountain

"In the days before tractors came into general use, one often heard old teamsters in the bunkhouse telling thrilling stories of runaway loads of logs on the steep hills.

"One of the devices lumbermen often use to get the heavy loads down the steep moutainsides is a steel wire cable which plays out over a series of pulleys. Some of these cables are over a thousand feet in length. The device, which is called a drum, is securely anchored at the top of some steep and dangerous hill. A man controls the action of the drum with a set of levers, and at any time could bring team and load to a complete stop even on the steepest hill. When the Santa Clara Lumber Company was lumbering in the Cold River country they used many of these drums to get the loads down the mountainside.

Early one morning before daylight, a load stood ready to be let down one of these steep roads. A man crawled under the load to hitch on the cable. Whether in the dark the man didn't get the key pin in the right place, or whether the clevis broke, or just what went wrong, I don't know that anyone ever knew. At any rate the team started the load but the cable didn't hold. The driver realized at once that something was wrong and rolled himself off the load and escaped. The team tried to save themselves by running but they were soon overwhelmed by the heavy load. Probably the load weighed over eight tons. There wasn't a semblance left of either horse. A jawbone of one of the horses was found stripped out and over thirty feet away from the road."

*　　*　　*　　*　　*　　*　　*

Logs Provide Safe Shelter

"Henry Kreuzer ran camps for many years, lumbering for the Hinckley Fiber Company. These camps were in the rough country along West Canada Creek. For many years Henry Kreuzer and Sol Carnahan had the reputation of being the best log drivers in the North Woods.

Mr. Kreuzer often laughs on recalling our first meeting in one of his camps not far from Nobleboro. Mr. Maddox and I had walked in together, I guess from Hinckley. Mr. Kreuzer had the reputation of getting an early start in the morning. The kerosene torches of his road monkeys could be seen bobbing along up the mountain side in the small hours of the morning. The weather, which had been quite cold, had changed and thick clouds and a rising south wind brought on a storm, half rain, half sleet.

"Of the several teams loading early at the rollways, Nick's team was the last one to start down. By that time the sleet had mingled with the sand on the hills. The shoes on Nick's sleigh runners were of a harder steel than usual, and altogther the prospects of his getting his load down safely from off the mountain were not good. The team and load kept on going faster and faster until the team, already on a run, failed to keep the road on a sharp curve, and ran out into the deep snow. The front end of the front bob sleigh struck a stump and the sleighs came to a sudden stop. The top tacklings on the load broke loose, and Nick and the top logs shot ahead over the team. Nick landed unhurt in the snow, far ahead

47

of the team. The front ends of the long 16-foot logs dropped into the snow ahead of the team, the rear ends of the log resting upon that part of the load which still remained on the sleigh bunks, just as they were when loaded. So there was the team, standing under a shed roof of logs.

"The loading crew came down and, with much labor and not a little skill, finally rolled the roof away. It was found that the only damage done was the breaking of two small straps. The only injury to the team was one slight cut on one of the horses, low down on a hind leg."

*　　*　　*　　*　　*

Sky Pilot Takes a Wild Ride

"One of Elbridge's boys, I think his name was Kenneth, was one of the teamsters. He was a tall, raw-boned, good-natured lad. He wore a big ten-gallon hat; in fact he was just the kind of fellow who, in the days of riding herd, would have been a cowboy. He would have been branding mavericks and riding bucking bronchos and bulldogging steers and all the other stunts of the rodeo. His was the lead team that morning. When he had his team hitched to the load, his father called to him and said 'Now you wait until the road men get the hills swept out.' 'All right,' he replied.

"For some reason, I wanted to get an early start that day and, as Kenneth climbed up on the front end of the load and hung his lantern up, I threw my pack sack up on the load and climbed aboard.

"The team started the load and we soon came to the top of the first steep grade, which had already been well swept out. We went along down that very well but there was a series of steep grades on that road a. d it was a good long way down to the bottom. While the sand hill men had been at work for some time they didn't have all the hills ready for the heavy loads.

"We were soon down to the place where the men were at work and I supposed that Kenneth would stop and wait, as his father had told him to do, but like a good many automobile drivers, he didn't wait a minute. He yelled at the road men to get out of the way, as they promptly did, and we flashed by.

"I never have been able to understand why we were not quickly upset. At several places the road crossed streams on narrow skid bridges. We came on to them by dangerously sharp curves. Time and time again we must have missed going off those bridges by only a very few inches.

" 'The team was utterly unable to hold the heavy load on the unguarded hills and were in a desperate run to save themselves. The load was swaying and pitching crazily from side to side. I am convinced that the only reason that we ever managed to keep in the road and keep right side up was that in a few places the grade was less steep and, once in a while the wind had evidently blown the snow out of the road and sleigh runners striking the sand, slackened our pace somewhat.

"When we finally reached level ground and could bring the load to a stop, Kenneth turned to me and said with a grin, 'If all of them get down as well as we did they will be all right.'

"The horses were in a lather and visibly shaking after their hard run. The T-bars in the bail chains of the harnesses each passed through two rings, and we found that on one of the harnesses the bar had slipped out of one of the two rings. If it had slipped through the second ring, I think nothing would have saved us from being sluiced. I was very thankful that we came out all right but it was one experience I should not care to repeat."

*   *   *   *   *

As Clarence Mason continued his ministry as sky pilot in the Adirondack lumber camps, he became increasingly recognized by the men of the woods for a variety of achievements.

They all considered him the oustanding Adirondack woodsman of his generation. He knew the Adirondack wilderness better than any other man and traveled long distances through the forest as well as over tote roads and trails. No other man of his time knew the Adirondacks as well as he. During his more than two decades of work in the mountains he travelled approximately 450,000 miles by automobile and 30,000 miles on foot often walking as many as thirty miles in a day to reach some isolated camp.

The men in the camps were keenly interested in the news which he brought from other camps and the outside world. This was before the time of the radio and communication was difficult. His news comments in camp laid the foundation for *The Lumber Camp News.*

All of the lumberjacks believed that he was interested in them and that his daily life was a striking example of Christian service. He took no offering in the camps. Why would he be taking these journeys except to share a great gospel and to reveal God's love for men?

The men were interested in the message he brought and expressed. He was not a ready speaker or a great orator, but his deeds gave an eloquence to his words which made them effective in the lives of men.

John Curry's Appreciation

John R. Curry thus expressed his appreciation of Mr. Mason's service in *The Northern Logger* of January 1958.

"He was gifted with a great faith and love of God and of the woods and he was most happy with the men who shared these loves. A simple humble man of God, he carried a great deal of the character of the Christ he loved and served so well. As Christ picked humble fishermen and farmers for his friends and disciples, Mr. Mason found no difficulty in exemplifying his Leader in his love and service for the humble and neglected lumberjack.

"Mason came swinging through the woods to Newtown's camp clearing at Bear Pond in midmorning one July day in 1922 where I was painting sleds. Having cut my knee wide open a week before, and this being before the days of compensation, I was working around camp. He was a fine looking man, six foot three or four, lean as a panther, and with a panther's easy lope. He had come, he announced, from Ed Brook's camp, on the Red River over in Moose River country, some five or six miles through the woods. I had never heard of the camp nor of the Red River. Our supplies were toted in from Raquette Lake and theirs from McKeever, I suppose. As far as we were concerned, they could have been in another world. Our peeled pulp was to be hauled to Raquette and shipped by rail to Glens Falls, theirs to be driven down the Moose to Lyons Falls.

"That day we talked and I learned a great deal, as I painted sleds, of an unusual man and unusual life. C. W. Mason on that July day in 1922 built into a boy not yet twenty a lot of himself which I hope to carry for my remaining years, as I have for the past thirty-five. I learned of principles of love and service which I hope to retain until I too am called. He was a quiet simple man of God with a great strength of mind and body to inspire men both young and old.

"Later, after supper, we held a meeting in the men's room. He talked first of the camps, where they were located, who was running them, of the cooks, and the bosses, and the strawbosses. This was of vital interest to the boys because lumberjacks have always been ready to move on. Wages were low in 1922, the year of the first postwar depression. Some of the boys were about ready to pack their pokes and go over the hill to a better job, and some of them did.

"Then he talked to us of the love of God and of the Commandments which He established; to follow which, would denote our love for Him. French, Irish, Russian, or plain American, we could all understand his simple message well."

Retirement and Death

Following his retirement on March 11, 1938, Clarence W. Mason continued to live in Ithaca, New York, just off the Cornell University campus. He maintained a keen interest in many activities. He was an entertaining and effective speaker for Boy Scouts, Men's Clubs and many other groups around the Ithaca area. He had many friends among members of the Cornell faculty. He read *The Lumber Camp News* with interest and wrote many articles which were of great interest to the men in the camps. On occasion, he went with his successor to Adirondack lumber camps, field days, and other activities.

He also did many things around the house which he had built at Ithaca years before, and shared occasional camping trips with his daughters, two of whom still live in Ithaca.

Mrs. Mason passed away in December 1945.

Mr. Mason died on October 12, 1957, and was laid to rest in the cemetery at Westmoreland, New York. The memory of him and his great service in the Adirondack lumber camps has lingered long in the minds of all who knew him.

Charles Atwood with pack-basket to carry his duffle. *(Photo courtesy Mrs. Alice Jones)*

Rich and Andrews General Store at Wanakena. *(Photo courtesy of Joseph King)*

Logging locomotive at Wanakena

Passenger coach from Benson Mines to Wanakena

Loading logs on railroad cars at Wanakena

Four-foot pulpwood above the mill.

Sky pilot Charles Atwood

William Empey's lumber camp on
Woodhull Creek near Forestport
(1922). *(Photo by Dewitt Wiley)*

Sky pilot Clarence Mason

Cutting a big pine at Bay Pond
on John E. Johnston job.

Big load of logs on landing.
(Photo by L. Beach)

A Linn tractor load and crew on Tug Hill.

Skidding logs at Bay Pond. Skidway is
located on log road for winter hauling.

V

FRANK REED

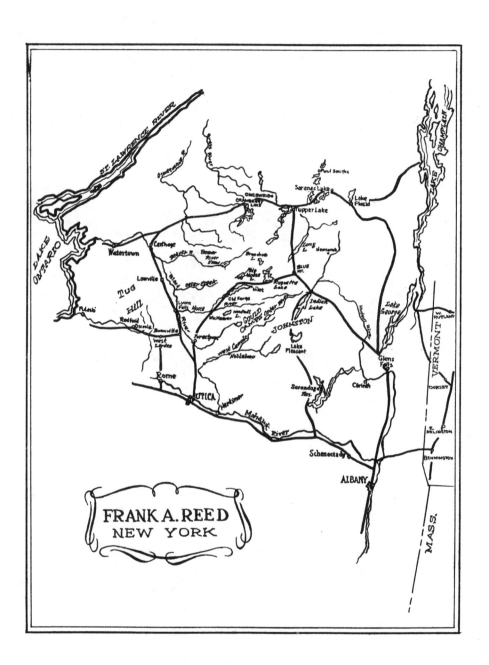

FRANK A. REED
NEW YORK

Frank Reed

EARLY YEARS

Boyhood Life in Southern New York

The writer joined sky pilots Aaron Maddox and Clarence Mason for his first visit to a lumber camp on April 16, 1917, and shared with them in a worship service at the bunkhouse in the John E. Johnston lumber camp on Woodhull Creek north of Forestport, New York. The crew at that season consisted of river drivers and mill employees at the neighboring sawmill. Men were friendly and gave close attention at the service which included a short sermon by the new sky pilot. One exception was a man who was partly intoxicated and occasionally interrupted with the comment, "That's right."

The new sky pilot's preparation for his task lay largely in the background of his boyhood experience. He was born and reared on a farm at Campbell, New York, which is located a few miles west of Elmira and not far from the Pennsylvania line. The farm house was the former home of the mill foreman in the Edward Armstrong mill which cut the virgin pine and hemlock in that area during the period 1866-1881. The hemlock also supplied great quantities of bark for neighboring tanneries.

Mr. Armstrong, like many other mill owners in the Northeast, operated his mill, at least in part, as an operation to clear land for farming. For that reason he completely cleared much of the land but did leave a six acre woodlot on the farm to supply fuel for the stoves. The cutting of the beech, birch, cherry, maple and oak for the wood supply was done on a selective basis to insure a long term operation.

The writer participated in all of the activities of the farm and woodlot including milking cows, plowing, harrowing, haying, cultivating potatoes, cradling grain and other duties. His special project was to keep the stoves supplied with sufficient wood. Familiarity with the axe, the bucksaw and the crosscut, as well as the grindstone and file, were experiences

55

which provided useful information in his later years in the Adirondack forest.

Walking two miles to school during most of his school career and five miles each morning and night in the later years of high school provided experience in hiking which was very useful in much longer hikes in later years over Adirondack trails and toteroads.

Plans for college work at Cornell University had to be postponed for lack of sufficient funds and the need of service on the farm. The alternative to college work was teaching in a one-room school, with the farm as the base of operations. One school had seven grades and the other eight, which made some planning necessary on class schedules.

The school teaching program gave way to operating the home farm. This was supplemented by some spare time work on a neighboring farm and in the anthracite coal business in town during the winter. Shovelling coal proved to be a muscle-builder if one were needed for a farm boy. One test of strength was to carry a three hundred pound barrel of salt.

The writer had his religious training in the Presbyterian Church at Campbell where Charles H. Bemis, John K. Ford, Edward Armstrong and other lumbermen of their day had participated actively in worship and leadership. He was especially influenced by pastor Robert Watkins, who had a keen interest in farm boys as well as village people.

A vital religious experience while at a convention in Wayland, New York, on April 28, 1914, led to plans for the Christian ministry. A correspondence course in Bible study gave some help in understanding the scriptures. Conducting services in inactive rural churches in the area gave the opportunity for constructive Christian service and on-the-job training.

An offer of the pastorate of a Methodist Church in a community near Keuka Lake led to an inquiry of the new pastor, Rev. Daniel Redmond, as to what opportunity the Presbyterian Church might have for a young man with some correspondence school training and experience in neighboring rural churches. Dr. Redmond suggested a letter of inquiry to Synodical Superintendent Dr. U. L. Mackey in New York City.

Dr. Mackey proposed the Adirondack lumber camps as the best opportunity and referred the inquiry to Rev. Aaron W. Maddox, who was senior pastor of the Adirondack Lumber Camp Parish with headquarters at Tupper Lake, New York. Mr. Maddox requested a meeting at the YMCA in Rochester in the late fall of 1916 and invited the writer to join the staff of the Lumber Camp Parish as soon as possible, with headquarters at McKeever. Other commitments prevented going to the Adirondack until the late winter of 1916-1917.

In the Adirondack Lumber Camps

The writer went to the Adirondacks on April 15, 1917, and was met at Remsen by sky pilots Aaron Maddox and Clarence Mason. He took part in his first service in a lumber camp bunkhouse on April 16th.

On the following day, Mr. Maddox introduced the new sky pilot to his headquarters in the lumbering village of McKeever. Headquarters consisted of a hotel room equipped with a small desk and a few books which he had brought from home.

McKeever was a thriving village at that time with a pulp mill operated by the Iroquois Paper Company and a big hardwood sawmill operated by the Moose River Lumber Company. Former Governor John A. Dix was active in the leadership of both mills. The Gould Paper Company of Lyons Falls had its woods headquarters at McKeever for extensive operations on the South Branch of the Moose River and neighboring areas.

McKeever was an excellent place for the on-the-job training of a new sky pilot. Logging activities were vigorous and manufacturing operated round the clock. Several men helped with information and other forms of assistance. These included John B. Todd, who was manager of logging operations for Gould; Mr. Brown, who was superintendent of the pulp mill; Forest Ranger Ed Felt; Edwin Kling of Taylor Crate, Inc., who was supervising the manufacture, grading and shipment of the lumber, and station agent Bernard Lepper, who arrived in McKeever on the same train with the sky pilot.

Religious services where held on Sunday morning at the schoolhouse in McKeever and on Sunday afternoons at the schoolhouse in Moose River which was five miles down the river. The method of transportation consisted of walking down the dirt road to Moose River and then another ten miles for an evening service in the rural church at Pinney Settlement which was a few miles from Port Leyden.

Adirondack Log Drives

The young sky pilot soon found that several interesting journeys were calling him to action. The first of these was to several river drives on streams in the western and central Adirondacks. The Gould Paper Company had three drives that spring: one on the Red River which was approached by way of Inlet and Limekiln Lake; one on the Upper Moose, which was about fifteen miles up river from McKeever over the toteroad; and one on the Lower Moose, which was about seven miles down the river.

Mr. Fuller was the driving foreman on the Red River and had to wait a few days for favorable wind on the ponds to start the logs. This gave the sky pilot an opportunity to get acquainted with the men. The foreman lost one man on the lower pond that year. The man lost his footing and went down between logs which closed over him so he couldn't come up.

William Mealus had a big crew on the Upper Moose to start the drive at the big landing and follow it down the Moose. Their next move after a few weeks was to the driving camp in McKeever. William's crew of rugged and experienced river drivers made the season without loss of life. The crew was very cordial to the new sky pilot who was making his first journey to river driving camps.

James Haley served as foreman of the driving crew on the Lower Moose, and used an old farmhouse for a driving camp. On the day of the sky pilot's visit, James said that two men fell into the river as they broke a center jam. They were able to pull one man out. The other, who had served for some years in the U.S. Navy and was a powerful swimmer, swam nearly across the river through rapid white water and made a safe landing. He participated in the worship service in camp that evening and was ready for a new day's work after breakfast. The worship service had meaning also that evening for foreman James Haley, who was thankful that his two men were safe in camp.

The John E. Johnston drive on Woodhull Creek above Forestport was a shorter but no less dangerous drive under the supervision of foreman William Empey of Forestport, who had his crew at the upper camp, which was also used during the cutting and skidding season. William's crew was made up mostly of men from the Black River area.

The river driving crew on the Beaver River was located at Soft Maple Dam which is not far from Croghan. The trip to this drive was made by way of the New York Central, the Lowville and Croghan Railroad, a three-mile walk and a boat ride across the pond. Charles Steinhilber, who was logging superintendent for the J. P. Lewis Paper Company, was in charge of this drive which brought pulpwood from the Beaver River Flow to the mill at Beaver Falls. Mr. Steinhilber and his men were very cordial to the young sky pilot.

The driving season journeys were completed that spring with a trip down Big Otter Creek from Thendara by way of Big Otter Lake. The crew was located in a driving camp at a place called Dolgeville on the Big Otter (not the Dolgeville near Little Falls.) This driving crew was made up largely of Black River men from around Lowville. The sky pilot will never forget the friendliness of the Big Otter crew and their close attention at the service that evening. One man was an Elder in the church at Lowville and was a friend of Aaron Maddox.

The driving season was completed by early May that year and was concluded with the loss of one man on the Red River. The crews had landed many thousands of cords of pulpwood at ponds above the mills for use during the coming months. The young sky pilot had found it to be an exciting experience. One striking fact was driven home to him from observation and experience: that the Adirondack wilderness was vastly different from the Steuben County woods which were interspersed with open fields. The traveller in the Steuben County woods would emerge in an open field in almost any direction while the traveller in the Adirondack wilderness might wander for a hundred miles if he was not familiar with his destination and possible routes of getting there. The map and the compass served as useful tools on such a journey.

As the season for felling the trees and peeling off the bark opened in early May, the woods along the Adirondack Division of the New York Central and for several miles back were alive with activity, which offered a challenge to the young sky pilot for a vigorous program of hiking and services in the camps. There were sixty camps in that area, with about three thousand men actively at work. The total Adirondack region had about one hundred and fifty camps with more than seven thousand men employed.

Lumber camps in the area were largely of log construction at that time. The combined cook camp and dining hall was a rectangular-shaped building of logs with several windows, a big stove, barrels for water, work tables for the cooks and several long tables for the crew. Meals there were well-cooked, with a large variety of food served on the tables. The diet included meat, potatoes, beans, other vegetables, home-made bread, some fruit, coffee or tea, pie and other desserts. Pancakes were a favorite at breakfast in the Adirondack camps. There was one strange thing about the meal in the cook camp. There was an unwritten law of the woods that meals would be eaten in silence except to ask for food. This law was strictly obeyed and was enforced by the cooks if any enforcement was necessary.

The bunkhouse was also a rectangular-shaped building built of logs and running in the same direction as the cook camp with a space between the two at the end. This space was covered over with a roof and was used largely to keep a supply of dry wood for the big stoves. The bull cook took care of the bunkhouse and kept a good supply of wood in the shed and in the bunkhouse for the day's use. The cookee was the cook's helper who washed dishes, helped with the serving at meal time and kept a supply of wood and water in the cook camp. He was often in training to become a cook.

The bunkhouse had a row of double decker bunks on each side except that space was left at one end for the sink, a barrel of water, the washbasins and a table where one might read, write or play a game of cards. A bench ran along each row of bunks on the inside. It was here that men sat in the evening facing the big box or barrel stove which kept the camp warm on the coldest nights. Garments hung on racks above the stove and under the bunkhouse roof.

The old-time lumberjack was a strong, rugged, highly-skilled man who was dedicated to his work. The bunkhouse was the old-time lumberjack's home. It was here that he slept, visited on winter evenings, sometimes played a game of cards on the table in one end, read a magazine which the sky pilot might have brought in his pack and wrote letters on occasion. His conversation generally revolved around the experience of the day on the job. The bunkhouse was also the old-time lumberjack's church on the occasions when the sky pilot came to camp. It was an informal service held at a convenient time in the evening when men were all in from the barn and included some news from other camps, the reading of scripture, a short sermon and a closing prayer. The sermon dealt with the Grace of God and the Power of Christ as the solution of vital issues in the lives of men and was illustrated with stories from the woods. Attention and participation were ordinarily excellent on the part of the crew. No offering was taken.

The rest of the buildings in the lumber camp included the barn, the blacksmith shop and the office. The barn was rather large in the day when the horse was such an important part of the lumbering program. The office was the foreman's headquarters where he kept his books and some vann for men. Vann included clothing, boots, tobacco, cigarettes and a few other things. The office was also equipped with a few beds for the foreman, the clerk, if there was one, and an occasional visitor.

A Journey on the Moose River

One of the sky pilot's early trips in May that year was to the Gould Paper Company camps up the Moose River from McKeever. Henry (Hay Wire) Hoe of Moose River had a camp on the north side of the river about fifteen miles in. The sky pilot's good reception at the camp indicated that the journey would be a pleasant one.

He visited two camps operated by James Canan on the south side of the Moose River and a few miles farther up. One of them was run by Joe Gordon and the other by Gardiner Poore. Joe Gordon was a young man, like the sky pilot, and had a crew made up largely of younger men, most of whom spent their lives in the camps. Ed Wheeler was the cook in one of these camps, and Mr. and Mrs. Holland, who lived near Lowville, were cooking in the other. Ed Wheeler came from Boston as a young man. A great sorrow in his early life sent him to the woods where he remained as a cook for the rest of his life and rendered excellent service. He became a very good friend of the sky pilot. Ed's major problems on journeys to the front were King Alcohol and too great generosity.

A visit to a camp run for James Canan by subjobbers Clinton and Walter Thompson near Stink Lake Mountain, led to a lasting friendship with the Thompson family who lived at Beaver River. The mother of the Thompson boys was the cook at camp and many of the crew came from Lewis County where the Thompsons had lived before moving to Beaver River. In later years, the sky pilot was called on to conduct the funeral services for both of the Thompson boys and their mother.

A hike through the woods to North Lake led to camps run by Frank Murphy and Doug Purcell of Lewis County for the Gould Paper Company. This job would later become a striking demonstration of careful planning and large scale execution on the hauling phase of the operation. On this trip the sky pilot met Rev. Byron Curtis, who had a camp on North Lake and was the author of the well known book, "Nat Foster."

A journey of some miles cross country and up river led to the camps of Lewis Joslin and his subjobber, Ward King, both of whom lived in Boonville. Mr. Joslin had his camp near the Upper Dam on the Red River while Ward King was near to the Lower Dam. Mr. Joslin was ably assisted by his son, Mort, who was a robust and vigorous young man in the woods and a lover of fast cars when he was outside. Mort's wife cooked for a time at camp.

The trail from the Red River led to Limekiln Lake and then to Inlet for the return trip to McKeever. The journey through the woods from McKeever to North Lake and Inlet had been about one hundred miles. However, the journey was not yet quite completed. Barnes and McGuire had a crew located in a large house in the village of Inlet and were operating in the woods near Eagle Bay. The crew, which was composed largely of men from the Boonville area, was very hospitable. Mrs. Barnes was the cook at camp with her daughter Harriett as the cookee. The presence of a young lady of Harriett Barnes' age as camp cookee was a bit unusual and might have caused a slight delay in the sky pilot's return journey. Harriett later married Vernon Sawyer and they set up housekeeping in Boonville where she now lives. Verne passed away in 1961.

The trip from Inlet to Old Forge was sometimes made on the steam-

61

boat and occasionally on the Raquette Lake Railroad from Eagle Bay. On this occasion, steamboats were not yet running and the train would not arrive for some hours. The fifteen-mile hike from Inlet to the railroad station at Thendara was interrupted by a man who was driving and asked the sky pilot to ride. He turned out to be a wholesale groceryman from Corning, New York, which was about twelve miles from the hiker's old home.

The territory north of Old Forge was alive with logging operations. George Vincent, who also had a hotel at Thendara, had nine camps around Carter and Big Moose for the International Paper Company. George Harvey acted as superintendent for Mr. Vincent with headquarters at Carter and Pat Harney served as head clerk. They had three camps on Independence Lake, one at Buck Pond near Big Moose, two on Twitchell Creek and some others. The crews in the Vincent camps were doing a tremendous job in getting out pulpwood for the International Paper Company.

The presence of Mr. Vincent's hotel at Thendara, where checks were cashed, might have been a temporary financial advantage to Mr. Vincent. It was a decided disadvantage to the men, many of whom went back to camp with only a headache to show for a week of hard labor.

The International Paper Company also had an operation at Woods Lake which was run by their subsidiary, the Champlain Realty Company. Headquarters was at Woods Lake where William O'Brien was superintendent, with Charles Fletcher as head clerk.

A railroad spur led down to a jack works on Twitchell Creek and a big camp with 112 men which was the biggest camp in the area. Ed Smith, who had been reared at Island Pond, Vermont, and had spent his life in the woods, was the foreman. Ed's opportunities for formal education might have been limited but he had a great knowledge of the woods, of logging methods and ways to handle men. He was also a practical joker, as shown by this incident. The young sky pilot had several hours to wait around camp and asked if there was something useful to do. Ed replied, "Yes, there is. Here is a pulp hook which you can use to help those two big Russians loading four-foot pulpwood in the box cars." The sky pilot helped the two men for about seven hours until the end of the day, had supper with the crew and conducted the religious service in the big bunkhouse that evening. It turned out that Ed did this as a practical joke. He thought the hard work on the pulp would leave the sky pilot too exhausted to conduct the service. However, work on the farm and shovelling coal had laid sufficient foundation for the necessary strength and endurance.

From that time on, Ed and the sky pilot were good friends. When Ed passed away at Old Forge some years ago, it was the sky pilot who was asked to conduct the funeral service.

Brandreth Lake Operations

Perhaps the busiest operation that year took place on the Brandreth tract at Brandreth Station and Brandreth Lake. Dr. Brandreth had purchased a tract of twenty-five thousand acres in 1851. Three of Dr. Brandreth's heirs had camps on the lake. These were: Ralph Brandreth, Colonel Franklin Brandreth and Annie Brandreth, wife of General E. A. McAlpine. Mr. and Mrs. Frederick Potter purchased the Ralph Brandreth camp in 1901. Mrs. Potter was Dr. Brandreth's granddaughter.

The operating company on the Brandreth Tract was Mac-A-Mac Corporation, which was composed of John MacDonald as President, Mr. McAlpine and Judge Abbott. Henry MacDonald was the head clerk while George MacDonald had a large camp in operation and Sandy MacDonald was the brakeman on the log train.

The Mac-A-Mac Corporation built a railroad from the station to Brandreth Lake and ran several spurs to other important loading areas. George LaFountain was the engineer on the log train with his son, Ernie, as the fireman.

The corporation had four large camps around Brandreth Lake, all of which landed their logs on the lake in winter. One of these camps was run by Leon Kelly, whose son Wilson has been manager of the Fish Creek Club near Boonville in more recent years. Other camps were run by Fred Baxter and Fred Johnson. Fred Johnson will be remembered best for hauling the champion load of logs in 1914. This load of sixteen-foot logs was loaded carefully on twelve-foot bunks. The load was about fifteen-feet high and was hauled to the landing by one team on a carefully iced road. The twenty-one and three-eighths cords of spruce on the load weighed approximately thirty tons.

Other camps on the Brandreth Tract were located on Lake Lila, at Little Rapids, Keep-A-Wa and other places. Cutting was done on a selective basis, with a diameter limit on trees cut. A border of two hundred feet around Brandreth Lake remained untouched. Colonel Brandreth had a deep appreciation of the forest on his tract and was one of the early advocates of Multiple Use, including scenic values, recreation, wildlife and forest products.

Trees on the Brandreth Tract, as in other places, were felled with a crosscut saw and peeled with a spud during the peeling season which ran ordinarily from May 15 to August 15. They were left on the ground at that time for later bucking and skidding. Activity in the late summer and fall included the layout and construction of winter road systems, bucking of the trees into logs and skidding them into big skidways along the log roads.

A major activity on Brandreth Lake in the early summer that year was the towing of log booms to the Jack Works for loading onto railroad cars. These logs had been landed on the ice in winter from the log jobs around the lake and were surrounded on each landing by booms, which were made by chaining logs end to end. When the ice cleared, they could be towed to the Jack Works with a small steamboat or gasoline launch, depending upon the size of the boom. They were loaded onto the cars with a log-length conveyor, which picked an entire log out of the water with hooks and carried it up the conveyor to a point where it dropped down on the railroad car.

The writer has a vivid recollection of two men in the Jack Works crew that year. Hugh McGillis was a big, strong and highly skilled man with years of experience in the woods and a very alert mind. He was a regular reader of the well known "Atlantic Monthly" magazine. He was also a frequent writer to the sky pilot during his service in the U. S. Army in World War I. Hugh later worked in a camp near Otter Lake but has not been seen in the Adirondack camps for some years.

John Watson who grew up at Watertown, New York, was also a skillful and industrious worker at the Jack Works. He came to the Adirondacks for his health but recovered sufficiently to become a woodsman. Mr. Watson later moved to Old Forge, where he served as a skillful carpenter and building contractor. He is still living there at the age of ninety-five.

The sky pilot conducted services on occasion at Brandreth Station and also among the summer campers and caretakers at Brandreth Lake. Everett Boyden of Crown Point, Wallace Emerson and Reuben Carey of Long Lake, and Ivan Stanton were caretakers at the time. It was here that the sky pilot met Mary Posson of Glens Falls, who was teaching the children at the lake and was a friend of the Boyden family.

Colonel Brandreth had a son, Courtney, who made frequent visits at the camp from the home at Ossining, New York, and a daughter, Pauline, who ran a farm at the lake. Occasionally the sky pilot lent a hand in digging potatoes or some other project. On one occasion, Miss Brandreth said she would have to bring in a blacksmith from Tupper Lake to put a couple of shoes on the horse. The sky pilot shod the horse so it was able to go about its work.

The J. P. Lewis Paper Company of Beaver Falls had two camps that year some miles north of the Beaver River flow. Logs from these jobs were later landed on the flow for the river drive to Beaver Falls. Mike Bush

64

operated one of these camps with John Backman as a foreman in the other.

The cook that year in Mike Bush's camp was a lady who was also a practical nurse. That talent was very useful on one occasion. A young man came into camp from the Croghan area for his first work in the woods. On the first day on the job, he was trimming the limbs from a tree which he had felled when the sharp double-bitted axe glanced and cut off one foot across the instep. The practical nurse administered first aid and dressed the foot well enough so he could ride on horseback to Stillwater and then by truck or automobile to the hospital.

The young man returned to work again after he had recovered and told the sky pilot an amusing story. He said a neighbor lady came in to make a call soon after he had returned to his home from the hospital. The neighborhood lady inquired, "Did you cut that foot off all at one blow?"

Cooties in Camp

Most of the Adirondack operators employed full time bull cooks who kept the bunkhouses neat and clean but they found the control of bedbugs and lice difficult before the days of DDT. Some did not employ bull cooks and made much less effort to maintain clean camps.

One Sunday afternoon the sky pilot hiked through the woods from Horseshoe to a camp on Round Pond Stream, which is south of Big Tupper Lake, and conducted a service in the camp that evening. This visit was to be the first one in the week's journey. The bunkhouse had the appearance of being poorly kept but didn't reveal the difficulties beneath the surface. In the darkness of the sleeping hours, the bed proved to be alive with both bedbugs and lice which tend to lighten the slumber and lengthen the night.

Under these conditions, the sky pilot changed his plans for the week. He hiked some miles to the railroad next morning and took the train back to headquarters at McKeever for a delousing operation and, then started on another camp journey.

The sky pilot made frequent trips by train from one logging area to another but more frequently "counted ties" and then hiked back to camp over the toteroad or trail or through open forest. During his years of ministry in Adirondack lumber camps, he "counted the ties" on the Adirondack Division from Forestport to Owls Head many times.

Services in the lumber camps were conducted during the week with other services at Beaver River, Brandreth and Carter on Friday or Saturday evening on the return trip by rail to McKeever for the Sunday program.

65

With the conclusion of the peeling season around August 15, the sky pilot began another series of journeys to the camps of the area. There were two marked differences in the season. The black flies, which had been a pest for all those who labored in the Adirondack forest during the period May 15-June 30, were now absent from the scene, which made both work and recreation much more pleasant. Horses came in great numbers for the skidding season and would continue to be the major factor in the winter hauling operation for some time to come.

Travelling in the woods is pleasant at most seasons of the year with the exception of the black fly season and periods when the toteroads may be muddy. The experience was especially gratifying in late September, when the temperature was moderate and the fall colors created many scenes of matchless beauty.

This was the season also in which road crews were busy laying out and constructing the road system for the winter haul. These road systems were laid out with gradual grades toward the landings, so that great sleigh loads could be hauled easily by the teams on the well-iced roads in winter.

The Winter Log Haul

The coming of the winter season ushered in a new season of labor for the old-time Adirondack lumberjacks. It came with a vengeance that year when temperatures dropped to 62° below zero on the Sunday morning after Christmas. However, the Adirondack operators were well prepared and welcomed a cold winter with sufficient snow to land the logs.

One early trip that winter led across the ice on Raquette Lake to the camp of Frank Newtown whose crew was housed in the little hotel at Marion River Carry. This was at the end of the shortest wide gauge railroad in the nation which carried people and freight from Raquette Lake to Eagle Lake and Blue Mountain in the summer season. There was no highway through that section of the Adirondacks at the time.

The icing of the roads for winter hauling was a new and interesting experience for the young sky pilot. With the coming of some snow and cold weather the men plowed out the roads with a Michigan or some other type of plow, then filled the huge sprinklers or water boxes at the water holes and put them on the log roads. At the proper spot the teamster's helper or whistlepunk would pull the plugs from the back end of the water box and let two streams of water run out onto the two sleigh runner tracks. They would continue this operation over the entire hauling road with other applications where necessary, until they had built up several inches of solid ice. This kind of road made good foundations over which

66

a team could haul a tremendous load to the landing. Experienced road-monkeys tended the road in sections during the winter and applied just enough sand to hills so that loads would move down without crowding the horses.

The most exciting haul that winter was in the Moose River-North Lake area where John B. Todd had planned to land the North Lake logs in the Moose River watershed. This involved some grades up hill in the early part of the log road which went over the edge of Ice Cave Mountain.

Mr. Todd began by constructing a hauling camp (Camp 7) near the summit and building a system of well-prepared and iced roads for the winter haul. He brought in more than a hundred teams for that operation and housed them comfortably in a large barn at Camp 7. As the haul opened, he stationed a few doubling teams at strategic places on the up-grade. Keeping a hundred teams moving smoothly in regular rotation during the hauling day required careful planning and real effort. Early teamsters and log loaders had breakfast at 2:30 a.m. and were out to the woods right afterwards, working with lighted torches. Other teamsters followed at regular intervals.

By 9 a.m. all of the teams were loaded and were on the way to the landing over the hauling road on this one-trip haul. Go-back roads were provided at least part of the way on the return trip so empty teams could meet the loaded sleighs. Early teamsters were back to Camp by 4 p.m. for supper, and all teamsters were in by 8:30. Ed Wheeler, who was cooking at the camp that winter, made the comment. "All I have to do from 9:30 p.m. to 1:30 a.m. is just sleep." Feeding a crew of hungry men at all hours made the cook camp a busy place.

The wood was landed successfully from North Lake at the big land-ing on the Moose River that winter. James Canan also landed his big cut of logs at the same landing. Henry Hoe used another landing on the north side of the Moose while Lewis Joslin and Ward King landed their logs on the upper and lower ponds on the Red River. These hauling op-erations were somewhat less difficult than the North Lake operation be-cause they could be done in two or three trip hauls each day.

One day in mid-winter the sky pilot was lending a hand to Shorty Cyr on the landing at the Upper Pond on the Red River and stepped down to straighten a log which had landed crisscross. Just at that time, a big log which Shorty Cyr rolled from his side of the bunk tipped the rest of the load in the opposite direction. A sudden yell of alarm on his part and a long jump into the snow bank cleared the way for the load of logs to land where the sky pilot had been a few seconds before. The size of the logs and load would have made it a fatal accident. Shorty Cyr continued to

67

serve in the woods for some years but more recently worked for many years in Boonville while the sky pilot has made his headquarters largely at neighboring Old Forge.

The winter hauling season was vigorous and successful that winter on all of the Adirondack jobs including those on Woodhull Creek, at Carter, Big Moose, Woods Lake, Brandreth, the Beaver River and other places. Cold weather and a good amount of snow were the elements necessary for success and they came in sufficient abundance for all of the operators to complete their hauls. The sky pilot found the roads suitable for hiking, the meals good, the bunkhouses warm, the crews friendly and the services in the bunkhouses well received.

However, as the end of the log haul drew near, it was evident to the sky pilot that he should be in the service of his country. He bade farewell to the neighbors at McKeever and in his home town at Campbell, New York, and entered the U.S. Army where he was assigned to a machine gun company with the infantry.

After a few weeks of training at Camp Dix, the division moved overseas. His particular part of it left in four ships from Montreal. These four joined many other ships off Cape Breton Island to form a convoy which travelled together for sixteen days across the Atlantic until one of them was attacked by submarines in the British Channel. There was no loss of life. A short stay in southern England was followed by a journey across the Channel to France for the rest of the war period.

On Christmas Day of 1918 the writer's regiment set sail on the Mauretania for New York and made the homeward journey in five and one-half days. The Mauretania then held the speed record for crossing the Atlantic. The last of the crew was discharged at Camp Dix on February 19, 1919.

Return to the Lumber Camps

After a few weeks at Campbell, New York, and a few visits in other places, the sky pilot returned to the Adirondacks and made his headquarters at Tupper Lake instead of McKeever where Stanley McKichen of Philadelphia, Pennsylvania, had replaced him.

Tupper Lake was a major lumbering center as it had been for many years and would continue to be. The Oval Wood Dish Corporation moved from Traverse City, Michigan, and had purchased large tracts of land in the northern Adirondacks. They built a large new plant on a site between Tupper Lake Junction and the village and opened extensive hardwood logging operations around Kildare under the supervision of Thomas

Creighton, who was the logging superintendent. This operation involved a rather extensive system of logging railroads.

Jack Bruce was foreman in one of the camps and Ed Smith, who formerly was foreman at Woods Lake, was foreman in another. Ed had a job which was extensive in both area and volume. During the sky pilot's visit to camp, a young man by the name of Martin Cummings came to get a job as filer and was successful in his mission. Martin was one of a large family of men, all of whom were active in the woods as blacksmiths and in other capacities. He had just returned from four years of service in the Canadian army.

One day some months later, Ed Smith's cook left camp and Ed said to Martin, "You are the cook here now." Martin has spent the rest of his life as a cook and most of it in the lumber camps. He has been living near Old Forge for the last twenty years.

Mr. Creighton was able to get out a good supply of logs from Kildare and other places to keep the Oval Wood Dish plant at Tupper Lake operating on a very active basis. It furnished employment to many people and has been a very important factor in the life of the Tupper Lake area. Mr. Henry S. Hull, who was then President of the company, was succeeded in 1920 by his son William C., who remained President of the company until 1941. He was succeeded by his son Gerald, who is now President.

The Racquette River Paper Company had two large pulpwood camps near the Oval Wood Dish Corporation camps back of Kildare. One of these was run by James Sullivan of South Colton. The crews in both of these camps were made up largely of rugged Russians who had left Russia in the period of the Bolshevik Revolution and had come to the Adirondacks. They knew very little English so communication in the religious services and in other contacts became somewhat difficult.

These men remained in the Adirondack camps. They learned the language and became excellent workmen. One logging operator later remarked, "If you want a job well done, get a Russian."

The logging program in the area north of Tupper Lake was somewhat less vigorous than it had been in the McKeever district. Charles Tate, who had come from Pennsylvania, had a camp near Piercefield. Clarence McCoy operated a mill at Pleasant Lake. There was a sawmill at Morgan's Siding near Lake Kushaqua. A pulpwood camp was in operation between Owls Head and Iron Mountain. Visits were made also to operations down the Beaver River and to a driving crew on the Saranac River.

The sky pilot's program that summer included some work in small communities and rural churches. This included the small village of Onchiota where religious services were held in a home, a girls' school at Santa Clara, a rural church at the Guide Board, where Dr. Harry Emerson Fosdick had been the summer minister for one or two summers, and some visits to the church at Paul Smith's where the sky pilot was entertained by Phelps Smith, the son of Paul.

That summer, the sky pilot married Mary W. Posson of Glens Falls and began housekeeping in a small house at Tupper Lake Junction owned by Thomas Banning. The next door neighbors, Mr. and Mrs. John Grant, and other neighbors were very cordial and made the Reeds feel very much at home. The journeys to lumber camps often led by way of large blueberry patches, where a pack basket could soon be filled with luscious blueberries. The six bushels picked that summer on camp trips furnished canned blueberries for the table over the next few years.

COLLEGE AND SEMINARY YEARS

Studies at Union College

At a meeting of the Adirondack Lumber Camp Parish staff in Tupper Lake in August of 1919, Synodical Superintendent U. L. Mackey suggested to the writer the advisability of pursuing college and seminary training and indicated that Union College in Schenectady, New York, might be a suitable place. A visit to the college showed that an examination in intermediate algebra would be necessary for entrance.

The examination was completed successfully at the college on a Friday afternoon in mid-September. The sky pilot spent Saturday digging his garden and packing, conducted the Sunday morning service in the Congregational Church in Malone, New York, and took the midnight train on Sunday for Schenectady. The train arrived in time for an eight o'clock class at Union College on Monday morning.

Married veterans of World War I were very much in the minority among college students at that time and had to support their families by the sweat of their brows. The writer did this by definite jobs each year.

He served as gardener at the college for the freshman year. The work included removing defective trees with the axe and saw in the fall and winter and the care of flower gardens in the spring season.

The extra curricular activity during the sophomore year consisted of work in a black varnish shop at the General Electric. Summer working hours were 7 p.m. to 5:30 a.m. while the working hours in the college year ran 7 p.m. until midnight.

A recession in 1921 brought a decline in employment at the General Electric and an experiment in private enterprise for the writer. He opened a pressing and cleaning shop near the campus to serve college students and other residents in the neighborhood. This turned out to be a successful operation.

A daughter, Winifred, came to gladden the Reed home on November 25, 1921.

Studies in the senior year at Union College were combined with parish activities as student pastor of the Presbyterian Church at Princetown which was ten miles out of Schenectady. The writer and his family lived in the parish manse and used a model T Ford for transportation about the parish and trips back and forth to college.

Close touch with the Adirondack lumber camps was maintained during the college years in Schenectady. The writer spent two summers in the lumber camps and in conducting services in the rural churches at Childwold and Stark which were located along the Raquette River between Tupper Lake and Potsdam.

At the close of the summer of 1923, the student minister and his family bade farewell to the kind friends and neighbors at Princetown and moved farther west to a new school and parish.

Auburn Theological Seminary

The school was Auburn Theological Seminary at Auburn, New York, which was a graduate school preparing men for the Christian ministry and the mission field. It also had a well known school of religious education for ladies.

The new field was a three church parish at Scipioville which was in an excellent farming area ten miles south of Auburn and included a number of highly intelligent, industrious and successful farmers. Most of the farms had been in the families for three generations or more. The farmers and village residents were people of fine integrity, a friendly Christian spirit and dedication to Christian ideals as well as their church. Their spirit was indicated by the action of one family who came to the manse on the first morning of arrival in town and said, "You people are to have breakfast at our house this morning."

The friendly spirit and fine cooperation of the Scipioville people made the ministry in that community a pleasant experience which has been remembered throughout a lifetime and has been a constant inspiration.

An Exciting Snowshoe Trip

The writer recalls several interesting events which took place during that period in southern Cayuga County. The most vivid recollection is of a three-foot snowfall which came in one night, paralyzing all kinds of traffic. Trolley cars and automobiles stood covered with snow in the middle of the streets. Trains were stalled and all highways were blocked. Many farmers had extreme difficulty getting to their barns.

Under these conditions, the student minister resorted to Adirondack methods. He waded to the hardware store, purchased a good pair of snowshoes, strapped them to his feet securely and began the snowshoe journey to his home twelve miles in the country. The snowshoes carried him out on the city streets, along the highway and across the fields where fences were completely covered with snow.

The light fluffy snow made snowshoeing difficult and progress slow. It was much like climbing stairs for twelve miles. However, the twelve mile journey was completed and the snowshoes were used to deliver groceries from the village store to a few people in need.

Most people in the countryside and along the way hadn't seen a man on snowshoes. Inside of three days the student minister was known throughout the county as the man who faced the blizzard on his snowshoes. This action would not have attracted attention in the North Woods.

The Reed family grew in numbers during their stay in the manse at Scipioville with the birth of Elwyn in 1924 and Ralph in 1926.

When the time of graduation drew near, four opportunities of widely different nature presented themselves to the writer. These included the Tea Pot Dome Oil Fields in Wyoming, a church in a suburb of Washington, D. C., a parish in Hawaii and the parish at Old Forge, New York, which was located in the heart of the Adirondack lumbering and resort area. Events seemed to indicate that the Lord's plan might be the parish at Old Forge.

Following graduation, the writer was ordained by his home Presbytery of Steuben in the church at Corning, New York. On June 1, 1926, he bade farewell to the good friends at Scipioville who had done so many kind things during his pastorate there and left for the new parish at Old Forge where he was installed on June 15.

RETURN TO THE ADIRONDACKS

The Village of Old Forge

The parish at Old Forge offered a great variety of opportunity. The village was the business center for a large area extending eastward

72

through the Fulton Chain of Lakes and Raquette Lake and north and south along the Adirondack Division of the New York Central.

The lake area around Old Forge had a large number of summer camps and hotels which were active during the period from June to September and entertained thousands of vacationists during that season. The resorts included the Adirondack League Club which had its headquarters at Little Moose Lake, three miles from Old Forge.

Many of the summer visitors were active church workers at home and shared actively in the worship services in the Old Forge area.

There were several new boys' camps near Old Forge. One of these, Adirondack Woodcraft Camps, which was organized and operated by William Abbott, recently celebrated its fortieth anniversary. Its growth and service have been very significant.

Niccolls Memorial Church at Old Forge, which was the center of the parish program, was organized in 1897 but moved to a new church building up the street in 1918. The new building was named in honor of Dr. Samuel L. Niccolls of St. Louis, Missouri, who had a camp on First Lake.

Many of the year round people of the community were engaged in serving the summer residents. Others were associated with sawmills in Thendara including George Deis and Company, Pullman Bros. and Lyon DeCamp.

The new minister quickly observed the absence of farms and farmers in the community.

Mr. Herrschoff, the pioneer who had founded the community, tried to develop iron mining and farming as the major activities but the winters were too long and the soil too thin for successful farming. When the mine at Thendara, as well as the farm, failed he ended his Adirondack itinerary by committing suicide. Since then no one has been foolhardy enough to take up farming in the area.

The Adirondack country has other important natural resources which include extensive forests, many lakes, rugged mountains, great scenic beauty and thousands of deer and other animals which roam the forest, as well as a variety of fish in the lakes and streams.

Small Railroad Communities

There were a number of villages along the railroad north and south of Old Forge which had several families and schools for the children. These communities had no churches or opportunities for religious training. It was logical that they become part of the Old Forge parish as the schools were part of the Town of Webb School system. Religious services were held in school houses and sometimes in barrooms. Many of the young

73

people who participated in these services are now active leaders in churches throughout the land.

There were also lumber camps in the parish including the Little Rapids Lumber Company hardwood mill and logging operations at Brandreth and operations at Big Moose, Woods Lake and Carter. Ed Smith also had a camp for Lyon DeCamp, north of Old Forge.

The beginning of work in a new parish made an ideal time to rethink the question of one's objectives in the Christian ministry. These were best expressed by Jesus himself on four occasions.

At the Well of Samaria He said to his disciples, "My meat is to do the will of Him that sent me and to finish His work." In His discussion on the Good Shepherd, He stated, "I came that they might have life and have it more abundantly." He summarized one section of the Sermon on the Mount by saying, "Be ye perfect even as your father in heaven is perfect," and another section of that sermon with this dramatic challenge, "Seek ye first the Kingdom of God and His righteousness and all these things shall be added unto you."

The doing of God's will, the perfecting of one's character, the enrichment of the lives of others and the seeking of the Kingdom of God were the major objectives in the life and ministry of Jesus. These make worthy objectives also for the followers of Christ and the Christian minister in his parish program.

Jesus' pursuit of these objectives in his own ministry brought a new concept of God and a fresh awareness of His presence in the lives of men. He gave men an experience of forgiveness for their sins and new power to conquer them. His life among men and His death on the cross were the world's most striking demonstration of the love that was both human and divine. He made his listeners aware of life's great objectives and ways to achieve them. He showed men the way to a greater fellowship in love which lifted them above petty jealousy and strife.

The ministry of Jesus provides both the inspiration and a dynamic pattern for the Christian ministry today whether it be in the church or the bunkhouse of a lumber camp.

Major features of the parish program at Old Forge were: an expanded program of worship services in the summer season, increased emphasis upon the education of children, an active youth program and extension of services into the small railroad communities and lumber camps. Worship services and church schools were conducted at regular intervals in the small villages. Frequent visits were made to the lumber camps to supplement the visits of sky pilot, C. W. Mason, who also made occasional visits to the church and manse.

74

In 1932, Big Moose Community Chapel asked the minister at Old Forge to serve that community also. This brought him into closer contact with the beautiful chapel which Earl Covey had built on the shore of Big Moose Lake and the Little Rapids Lumber Company camps at Big Moose.

The summer minister at the time at Big Moose Chapel was Dr. J. Hillis Miller, President of Keuka College, who was a friend of the winter pastor. The two ministers cooperated closely in the service of the Chapel. Dr. Miller was later Associate Commissioner of Education in New York State and President of the University of Florida. Dr. Thomas Wearing, Dean of Colgate-Rochester Seminary, succeeded Dr. Miller as summer pastor at the Chapel. Methodist Bishop Fred G. Holloway has been the more recent summer minister.

The Central Adirondack Larger Parish

Early in 1936, the churches at Inlet and Raquette Lake invited the Old Forge minister to serve as pastor of the these churches also, for a time, along with the churches at Old Forge and Big Moose

This latter service led to the cooperation of all four churches in establishing the Central Adirondack Larger Parish with a Governing Board of church officers to guide the parish program. The winter staff consisted of one full-time minister, with some additional help in religious education and secretarial service. The summer staff included two additional ministers and a summer director in religious education.

One major feature of the parish program was the Central Adirondack Youth Council which included about eighty young people and carried on a very active program. Many of these young people have become active church leaders in their communities.

One of the minister's visits to a lumber camp during this period brought an unusual type of experience. Cards were the major form of recreation in the lumber camps. Men who worked hard in the woods didn't need active sports to give them exercise. Ordinarily the card game was a quiet one for fun in the bunkhouse in the evening and involved only a few men.

A call was made to George Bushey's camp at Woods Lake one day and the minister took a walk around the job with the foreman, who was a Frenchman recently from the Province of Quebec. The minister asked about the possibility of a religious service at the bunkhouse in the evening and received the new foreman's consent.

After supper the foreman and some of the crew started a big poker game on the bunkhouse table. Interest in the game grew as the values of the stakes increased. Members of the crew who were not playing watched the game with interest as they stood around the long table in the bunkhouse behind the players.

When the hour of 7:30, which was the usual time for the religious service, arrived the interest of the foreman and other men in the poker game seemed to be waxing keener. The sky pilot asked the foreman, "When shall I speak to the men?" The foreman replied, "Why don't you do it right now?"

The players pushed their cards toward the center of the table and looked toward the speaker at one end. One of them had a big heap of bills in front of him. Other members of the crew stood in back of the players as they had been doing while the sky pilot conducted the service, including a short sermon. Attention and interest were excellent. This was the only time that the sky pilot ever delayed or broke up a big poker game to conduct a religious service.

Old Forge was fortunate in having two well-qualified physicians who cared for the health of people many of whom came to the mountains for health reasons.

Dr. R. S. Lindsay came to the community from Lockport, N. Y., in 1902 for Mrs. Lindsay's health and served many neighboring lumber camps, as well as the people of the community for many years. In 1925 his son, Dr. R. N. Lindsay, became associated with him and later took over the practice which he has carried on effectively until the present time. Dr. R. S. Lindsay passed away in 1938 and Mrs. Lindsay in 1949.

Dr. S. W. Nelson, who had been reared in Taberg and Boonville, New York, came to Old Forge in 1897 for health reasons. He soon recovered his health and began medical practice in the community. His medical service included visits to villages along the railroad and to many lumber camps in the area which he reached by hiking over the toteroads.

An Unusual Accident

Dr. Nelson tells an interesting story of an unusual accident which took place at the Pullman Bros. mill years ago. George Lanz, who was the edgerman in the mill, lifted a spruce edging which was stuck on the saw. As it came free, the swiftly-revolving saw caught it again and sent it like a bolt of lighting. The thirteen-foot edging pierced Mr. Lanz's chest and came through on the right side of his back, also piercing his right arm.

Members of the mill crew carefully sawed both ends of the thirteen-foot piece so Mr. Lanz could ride in the baggage car. He was treated by

76

Dr. Nelson who accompanied him on the train to St. Elizabeth's Hospital in Utica.

After careful examination, Dr. Hyland, a prominent surgeon on the hospital staff, decided to remove the edging through the back and proceeded to do so. George Lanz recovered and had many useful years of service. His son, Frank Lanz, is an experienced printing pressman at the Willard Press in Boonville and has printed most of this book.

During the pastorate in Old Forge, the Reed family was blessed with the arrival of its third son, Frederick who was born in September, 1929. This was the month before the stock market crash and the beginning of the Big Depression. Frederick is now a minister in Kentucky.

The minister has many fine memories of years in the Old Forge, Big Moose and the Central Adirondack parish, including a deep appreciation of the friendliness and cooperation of people. He recalls one experience which was particularly amusing. On a call in an Old Forge home, he observed that the furniture had been moved around the living room since his last call and remarked about it to the lady of the house. She replied, "I would like to move the furniture around every week to make the room look different but my husband objects to that. However, I told him that, as long as I take my desire for variety out on the furniture, he shouldn't mind."

FULL-TIME SKY PILOT

With the retirement of sky pilot C. W. Mason on March 11, 1938, which was his seventieth birthday, a committee of men from the Synod of New York was chosen to study the program and secure a replacement. Rev. A. W. Maddox was still active but advancing years made the woods trips somewhat difficult for him. The writer was a member of that committee which made inquiries in many lumber camps and among foremen, superintendents, operators and company executives as to the value of the ministry in the camps.

The large number of enthusiastic replies by person and by mail indicated that the ministry of sky pilot C. W. Mason had been a very fruitful one. Men regarded him highly, not only as the best woodsman of his time in the Adirondacks, but also as a sincere Christian who had a keen interest in the men and had done much to make their lives more abundant.

Members of the committee turned to the writer and said, "You are the only younger man who has had experience in the camps. You should take up the work which Mr. Mason has left." After some weeks of consideration, the writer resigned as minister of the Central Adirondack Larger Parish and, October 1, 1938, resumed his ministry as fulltime sky pilot to Adirondack lumberjacks. He moved from Old Forge to Boonville where he made parish headquarters for the next four years but later returned to Old Forge.

As the passing years made woods travel somewhat difficult for Mr. Maddox, he was made responsible for work in small villages and rural communities and the writer for service in lumber camps of the Adirondacks and on Tug Hill.

Birth of "The Lumber Camp News"

During a visit to Bid Harvey's camp at Nobleboro in October, 1938, Bid's cousin, lumberjack Ross Harvey, made the statement to the sky pilot in the presence of lumberjack Jerry Ryan, "we ought to have our own newspaper in the camps." The suggestion grew out of work which Mr. Mason had done as a walking newspaper in the camps.

The question of a newspaper in the camps was discussed in other camps and received favorable reaction. As a result, the "Lumber Camp News" was published during January, February and March, 1939, on an experimental basis. Three hundred copies of a four-page paper were printed by Ira Cope of Old Forge at a cost of ten dollars per month.

By the end of the log haul in March of 1939, the sky pilot had three hundred paid subscriptions in the Adirondack and Tug Hill lumber camps. It began regular publication in May, 1939, and has had monthly publication since that time.

When the sky pilot took up his full time duties in October, 1938, he discovered that several changes had taken place in the parish program since his early trips twenty-one years before.

He had served camps in specific areas such as the southwestern or northern Adirondacks in the early years and in later camp visits. He discovered that his parish now included the entire Adirondacks, the Tug Hill area west of the Adirondacks and the John E. Johnston operations in Vermont. The coverage of this broader area was made possible by the fact that some new roads had been built and all roads were plowed in winter so one could make fuller use of automobile transportation. The sky pilot might have a hike of three or twenty miles to camp from the nearest highway but he could travel to the general area by car at all seasons of the year. This eliminated the necessity of travelling all winter on snowshoes as Clarence Mason had done in earlier years.

The car made a base of operations for camps in a specific area. One could carry snowshoes for use on winter trips, hiking boots for muddy toteroads in other seasons of the year, jackets suitable for weather conditions, a pack for supplies on camp trips, a suitable supply of magazines, New Testament gospels and other things which one needed for the camp journey.

The number of camps was somewhat reduced. It had declined from its high peak of one hundred and fifty in the World War I period to about twenty at the depth of the depression in 1933. The number was on the increase again in 1938 and would reach sixty camps by 1940 with about three thousand men employed.

Most of the Adirondack lumberjacks were the same men with whom the writer had been associated two decades earlier but, like himself, they were a few years older and more experienced. The crews were still made up of Northern New Yorkers, Canadian French, Finns, Irish, Lithuanians, Russians, Scotch and Swedes. There were an increasing number from Northern New England, Pennsylvania and West Virginia as the logging program expanded.

COMPANY OPERATIONS

Several lumber and paper companies in and around the Adirondacks carried on their own logging and pulpwood operations from their own lumber camps. Part of the men in their crews did the felling, peeling, bucking and skidding on a piecework basis. The list of these companies in 1939 included:

Gould's Moose River Operations

The Gould Paper Company of Lyons Falls, New York, had extensive forest land holdings on Tug Hill and the South Branch of the Moose River. Pulpwood from the South Branch was driven to the mill on the river in the spring season. The company made use of Fish Creek in the Tug Hill area for a river drive and used trucks from the jack works to replace the Glenfield and Western Railroad which had formerly furnished the means of transportation.

The Manager of Woodlands for the company was Gordon Gould, son of President Harry Gould, who had succeeded John B. Todd. A short time later Harry Gould died and was succeeded by his son, Gordon, as President. Roy Bird was then made woodlands manager and served in that capacity for a year or two. The superintendent of the Gould operations on the Moose River was Hugh Dowling, who came from Croghan and spent most of his life on the Moose River.

The returning sky pilot soon made a trip to the Gould Paper Company camps on the Moose River. The foreman at Camp 1 was Charles McVey, who had worked on the Moose River operation back in 1917 and for many years afterwards. Many of his crew had also worked on the job in earlier years. Charles and his men were very cordial and attentive at the service in the bunkhouse. They became enthusiastic supporters of the "Lumber Camp News."

Levi Godin was the foreman at Camp 2, which was nineteen miles in from the highway and two miles beyond Camp 1. Many of Levi's crew were also men who had worked for years on the Moose River operations. Levi went into the woods in early May, stayed through the summer, fall and winter and went down with the drive in the spring. After that he spent some time at his home in Canada and in Tupper Lake. When in Tupper Lake, he was the best dressed man in town.

The visit on the Moose River in the autumn season indicated that only a few changes had been made in method from earlier years. The crosscut was used for feeling and bucking as it had been earlier. The horse was used for most of the skidding.

The camps were built of logs in about the same form as they were two decades before.

Herbert McGhee, who was foreman at the road camp, was a former Canadian who had come to work on the river drive for the Gould Paper Company back in 1916 and spent most of his life on the Moose River. Herb was made foreman of Camp 3 in 1940 and continued to serve as foreman for several years including leadership on the river drive. He lived at Turin, New York.

Herb had a variety of men in his crew including several Indians from the Hogansburg Reservation in Northern New York. The best known man of this group was Mike Solomon who was a graduate of Carlisle University in the class with the famous athlete, Jim Thorpe. Mike had several children who were serving in good positions outside the woods. Following the death of Mrs. Solomon, he returned to work in the woods where he had had his roots as a boy. Mike was a skillful road monkey on the log haul and often acted as lawyer and interpreter for his colleagues from the Hogansburg Reservation.

The sky pilot became well acquainted with Mike and saw him occasionally outside as well as often at camp. On the last such occasion, Mike crossed the street in Boonville and said, "Hello, Mr. Reed. How are you? I owe you five dollars and here it is."

The key man in Herb's crew was "Scotty" Hill who sharpened and tempered the steel drills for road construction in his blacksmith shop at camp. "Scotty" had come from Scotland by way of South Africa where he fought in the Boer War. He worked in steel plants for some years and was the Adirondack's most highly skilled man in tempering steel drills. Lucky, indeed, was the road crew which had "Scotty" Hill as its blacksmith.

"Scotty" became a good friend of the sky pilot who often held mail and packages for him sent by his sisters in Schenectady. He was a frequent visitor at the Woodsmen's Club but later retired and went to live with his sisters in Schenectady.

A visit to the Gould Moose River operations in the following winter hauling season indicated some important changes which had taken place in transportation since earliest days on the Moose. In fact, John B. Todd had introduced these changes back in the World War I period. He had said to Mr. Linn of the Linn Tractor Company of Morris, New York, in the fall of 1918, "If your tractor will haul as many logs as twenty teams, I will buy three of them." Mr. Linn came into the woods and demonstrated that his tractor could do the work of twenty teams. John B. Todd purchased three for the hauling season of 1918-19, which were later replaced with bigger ones. The Gould Paper Company purchased four sets of these machines. The last set was a group of very powerful machines which hauled trains of log sleds much like a railroad engine. The Linns had sleigh runners in front for steering and were particularly useful for trains of logs on the long hauls. Surplus tanks after World War I had also laid the foundation for the use of crawler tractors, particularly for yarding the logs.

Gould's Tug Hill Camps

A visit to the Gould Paper Company operations on Tug Hill led to some interesting experiences. Tug Hill is the greatest snow belt of New York State as the sky pilot soon discovered from occasional forced stopovers in the area on account of drifting snow. Elmer Bernier was the big operator in the Tug Hill area in cooperation with John E. Johnston. Elmer was an efficient operator who always had his machinery in order and his job well planned.

Elmer had a foreman by the name of Joe Morin who had formerly worked with him as a lumberjack in the woods. Both were natives of Canada where they had become familiar with logging and river drives. Joe was an exceptionally industrious man who was up early in the morning before the crew arose in order to have everything ready for the day's

81

operation. He was a very skillful river driver and an excellent all-round lumberman.

Joe was fond of photographs and particularly moving pictures. He would collect funds among the men to purchase film so the sky pilot could take movies of the job and run them in camp. They often furnished an evening of entertainment for his own and other camps. They have also been run scores of times in schools, churches, service clubs and other places. The four thousand feet of colored movies now on hand give an exciting story of Adirondack and Tug Hill logging. Joe and Elmer later moved to Nobleboro to log pulpwood on the West Canada.

Elmer Bernier had two well known men in camp by the name of Frank. Frank Allain came from the Province of Quebec with Elmer and Joe Morin and worked for several years on Elmer's operations. He married Mrs. Bernier's sister and made his home in Boonville for some years.

Frank McCarthy was of Irish extraction as his name indicates. He was a highly skilled and industrious lumberjack who was very witty and had a voice which could be heard a quarter of a mile. Frank was the life of the bunkhouse when he was in camp. His drinking habits of earlier years gave way to complete sobriety in later life. Frank passed away in 1956 and was laid at rest in St. Joseph's cemetery in Boonville where a gray granite monument carries his name along with those of several other old-time lumberjacks.

Both the Moose River and Tug Hill operations had extensive log drives in the spring season when the rivers were high. Hugh Dowling and Herb McGhee were in charge of the drive on the Moose while Joe Morin was the river driving foreman on Tug Hill. These operations produced and used large crews of highly skilled log drivers and boatmen.

As Elmer Bernier moved the scene of his logging operations from Tug Hill to Nobleboro, John Hogan of Osceola, who had spent his life in logging in the Tug Hill area, became superintendent of Gould operations in Tug Hill. Headquarters camp was located a few miles northeast of Osceola with other camps in the surrounding forest. Joe McDermott of Port Leyden moved from the Moose River country to help John Hogan in the program. John and Joe also operated for some time for the Adirondack Core and Plug Company of Carthage, New York.

George Colvin of Redfield, New York, also became an extensive operator for the Gould Paper Company in their tract near Redfield. George introduced a new method in using the brooks as log roads in the summer and autumn season. He purchased a large tract of land on the Raquette River near South Colton and moved his operations to that area.

Finch, Pruyn Camps at Newcomb

In 1938, Finch, Pruyn and Company had extensive operations under logging superintendent Charles Treggett at Newcomb and on the Cedar River. Mr. Treggett had his headquarters at the Farm near Newcomb where the company had large horse barns, a pasture, an office, a dining room and rooms for guests.

At that time, the company was operating seven large camps with combined crews of about five hundred men and hundreds of horses in the skidding and hauling season. Mr. Treggett's son, Jack, had a large log camp near Boreas Ponds. His camp was equipped with single bunks in double decker style and shower baths. An inquiry indicated that all of the men in camp used the shower. Jack was proud of his camp and a well run job.

A six-mile hike from Jack's camp to Boreas Mountain on the other side of the pond led to the operation and camp of Carl Linstrom. Carl had come from Finland some years before and had worked for William Eggleston at Brewer, Maine, before coming to Newcomb. Carl had a crew composed largely of Finns and was working on very steep country. He made use of cables and drums to brake the sleigh loads on the steep mountains. Carl also had a well equipped camp but the Finnish steam bath took the place of the shower.

Osias Tellier had a camp on the side of Santanoni Mountain with Henry Fenger as assistant foreman. This job was not as steep as Carl's job on the Boreas but required much hiking over the hillsides. Mr. Tellier's camp was also equipped with showers. Ernest Allie, who made his home in North Creek, had a large and well equipped camp on Beaver Brook.

All of the wood at Newcomb was bucked into four-foot length in the woods during the skidding season. The skidding was done in tree-length to a landing and then bucked and piled along the hauling road.

In the winter season, the crews iced the roads carefully as they did on the log jobs and hauled the pulpwood to the landings on the lakes and rivers with horses. The hauling season was a busy one involving an early breakfast and long days of work for both men and horses.

Melting snow and rain in the spring season raised the water in the streams so the four-foot pulpwood could be driven down the Boreas and other tributaries into the Hudson River and down to the mill in Glens Falls. Jack Donahue was the superintendent on the drive.

Jack Donahue told the interesting story of a visit to the driving camp on the Hudson by sky pilot Clarence Mason. Mr. Donahue said to Mr. Mason on the evening of his visit to camp, "Mr. Mason we have had quite a dry spell and need rain badly to complete this drive; if you have any influence with the powers that control the rain, please remember us." The crew retired to their temporary bunks which were made up on the ground in tents. During the night, the rain came down in torrents so Mr. Donahue and crew were awakened and had to dig trenches around the tents to keep the bunks and themselves dry. Mr. Mason inquired of Mr. Donahue the next morning, "Was that rain satisfactory?"

Finch, Pruyn and Company operated two large camps on the Cedar River above Indian Lake. One of these was run by Joe Paradis, who had come from Canada and lived at North Creek. On the occasion of the sky pilot's visit to Joe's camp, the teamsters went on a strike for higher wages. This was the only strike which the sky pilot ever witnessed in the camps. Several of the teamsters walked out the next morning with the sky pilot as he headed for the next camp. The joke was on the teamsters, however. The temperature stood at 45° below zero and none of the cars would start.

The second camp on the Cedar River was run by Henry Savarie of Indian Lake, who had spent his life working in the woods in that area. Henry had a well-built camp for a crew of eighty men. It was well-lighted and equipped with running water and showers. One of Henry's lumber-jacks was Big Mike, the Russian, who always took the company prize for the best cut and piled work. Big Mike's daily production in the skidding season ran from eight to ten cords and he took real pride in having beautiful piles along his section of the log road.

Before the return of Finch Pruyn and Company to the Cedar River country, Henry Savarie was a foreman for the Union Bag Company in remote camps up the Cedar River. Mr. Mason visited the Union Bag camps by crossing through the woods from the Gould Paper Company operations. This was the most remote area of the Adirondacks.

Henry Savarie told the story of a visit by Mr. Mason to the camp far back during the hunting season. A hunter became lost that afternoon some miles from camp and Henry took some men from the crew in the evening to find him. Mr. Mason went along on the trip. They finally found the lost hunter some distance from the Henry Savarie job. The question then was, "Where is camp from here?" Mr. Mason said, "Follow me, I'll lead you back to camp." He had frequently checked directions on his compass as they went in search for the lost hunter. Henry Savarie agreed with many other old woodsmen that sky pilot Clarence Mason was the best woodsman in the Adirondacks in his generation.

One evening in a camp on the Cedar River the sky pilot went about the bunkhouse after the service visiting with men before they retired for

Loading logs at skidway on
Woodhull Creek (1918).

Frank Reed on the top of
Mt. Marcy (1927).

Breaking wing jams on the log drive

Larry Muggins at Lower Woodhull Creek camp — 1919. *(Photo
by Dewitt Wiley)*

Loading logs at the jack works. Logs have been driven and boomed to this point.

Bill Hutchins ices the road with big
water box or sprinkler.

Logs at the hardwood mill in McKeever—1916.
(Photo by Ed Kling)

Skidding and hauling horses on George Colvin job

Skidding peeled pulpwood logs
on Gould Paper Company job
(1947)

Hauling logs with Linns on Elmer
Bernier's Tug Hill job—1939.

Gould Paper Company's last drive
on the Moose River (1948).
(Photo by Fynmore)

Clarence J. Strife plans a
logging operation (1949).

Loading pulpwood on Finch, Pruyn and Company job.   *(Photos by Fynmore)*

Logging operator George Colvin (left) and foreman
Ernie Hebert plan logging job.

the night. One man on a lower bunk was reading a book. Closer scrutiny of the book indicated that the title was, "The Complete Works of Victor Hugo." The sky pilot observed that this lumberjack had a shelf of books over his bed including "The Complete Works of William Shakespeare" and several other well known authors. He had purchased them in New York City at $1.89 each and was reading them during odd spells in camp.

Finch, Pruyn and Company was carrying on a constructive forestry program on their extensive land holdings under the supervision of Thomas Crashaw who was a graduate of the University of Maine and an outstanding forester. Tom made use of forestry students during the summer season and started many a young man on a successful career. His forestry crew marked the trees which were to be cut in an area before the logging crews moved in.

Louis Seheult succeeded Charles Treggett as logging superintendent in 1945. His coming marked a change in logging method on the Finch Pruyn operations. Mr. Treggett had served the company effectively for many years with the tools of the passing generation including a large number of horses. The younger man, Louis Seheult, was looking toward the future and increased the momentum of the mechanization program including the use of the chain saw, the bulldozer and other mechanical equipment. He was encouraged in this program by the company's new President, Lyman Beeman, who succeeded Maurice Hoopes in that office in 1949. They experimented also with a Wyssen Cableway but found it impractical for Adirondack logging.

Louis Seheult went to the University of New Brunswick in 1950 and has served there as Professor of Logging since that time.

When Thomas Crashaw died in 1947, he was succeeded by Robert Whyland and, after Mr. Whyland's death in 1963, by Norwood Olmstead who is now the woodlands manager.

W. E. Ward

W. E. Ward operated a sawmill for several years on the Cedar River and carried on his own logging operations. He ran a family type of camp and housed his employees with their families in a small village near the mill.

Mr. Ward later moved his office to Minerva, New York, and the mill to the Sanford Lake area a few miles away.

Following the death of Mr. Ward, his daughter Eva operated the mill with Sid Lawrence as superintendent of both mill and logging operations.

The Emporium Forestry Company

The Emporium Forestry Company had a hardwood band mill at Conifer which is near Tupper Lake. They had closed the mill at Cranberry Lake but were still operating the railroad.

George Sykes had succeeded his father as president of the company with his brother Clyde as secretary and treasurer. Victor Noelk was logging superintendent with John Stock joining him a little later as assistant superintendent. Most of their logging was done by contractors.

The Emporium made a large sale of seventy-five thousand acres of forest land to the Draper Corporation in 1945. This sale came at the time when the Draper Corporation was planning to build a new mill at Tupper Lake to produce bobbins for their textile equipment and other lumber products. The mill was opened in 1948.

Farrell Lumber Company Mill

Gerome Farrell was operating a big hardwood mill at Poland, New York, and securing his logs from a large tract of forest land at Nobleboro on the West Canada Creek. Bid Harvey was superintendent of logging operations. It was at this camp where Ross Harvey made his suggestion about the Lumber Camp News.

Mr. Farrell sold his mill in 1945 to George Kingsley who added much modern equipment and renamed it "The Northern Lumber Company." Mr. Kingsley later established a mill at Riverside, New York. These two mills make Northern Lumber Company the largest hardwood operation in Northern New York.

The Oval Wood Dish Camps

The Oval Wood Dish Corporation at Tupper Lake, New York, had reduced its annual cut since the high production period of 1919 to conserve raw materials. They had operations under way on their own lands at Kildare and Parishville under the general supervision of logging superintendent Thomas Creighton. The staff of foremen included Bert Frank of South Colton, Con Buckley of Irishtown in the eastern Adirondacks and Edmund Tope of Tupper Lake. Bert Frank and Con Buckley had served as foreman with the company for many years.

Roy Lavoy joined the logging staff in 1919 as clerk. He was made assistant superintendent to Thomas Creighton in 1945 and became logging superintendent in 1952 when Mr. Creighton retired. Roy passed away in 1953.

Elliott Hardwood Operations

Clayton Elliott, who had moved his mill operation from Coudersport, Pennsylvania, to North Creek in 1913, and later to Tupper Lake, moved to Potsdam where he installed a new hardwood band mill in 1930.

North Siglin of Childwold, New York, was the superintendent of logging operations for the company and was cutting logs in the Tupper Lake area.

The Elliott Hardwood Company has continued to be a large producer of Adirondack hardwood. Following Clayton Elliott's death in 1951 his son, Basil, became President of the company with his grandson, Richard, also playing a prominent role.

Julius Breckwoldt

Julius Breckwoldt purchased a plant at Dolgeville, New York, from Alfred Dodge in 1900 and continued to operate it until 1943 when he sold it to Claude Johanssen. Mr. Johannsen died in 1953 but his family has continued to operate the mill until the present time. Bernard A. Wein was made General Manager in 1950 and the name of the company was changed to North Hudson Woodcraft Corporation.

This mill specializes in piano sounding boards from choice Adirondack spruce. Sounding boards for grand pianos are made from select trees where the heart is off center, causing the growth rings to be nearer together on one side. This is the kind of Adirondack spruce tree which furnishes the material for the grand piano used by Liberace.

Bernard Wein considers the choice of the spruce tree so important that he spends much time in the woods on the search for these select trees. The desired material is cut by a combination of company and contract operations.

Adirondack Bats

E. D. McLaughlin and Hal Schumacher of Dolgeville, New York formed Adirondack Bats in 1946 to manufacture baseball bats for both the big and little leagues. Mr. McLaughlin, who brought his background of experience in wood manufacturing, became President of the company while Hal, who was a successful pitcher for the New York Giants, was made the Sales Manager.

The company used quality ash in 40-42 inch bolts to manufacture the bats for use by many of the batting stars in the big leagues. They supplied these bolts by various methods including contract operations and a purchase program in the Adirondacks and company operations in Northern Pennsylvania.

87

The Frank S. Harden Company

The Frank S. Harden Company was founded at McConnellsville, New York in 1883 and has been engaged in the manufacture of solid cherry furniture. The company has its own sawmill which saws the cherry logs into proper dimensions.

Log supply for the mill has been provided by a combination of company and contract operations, together with a purchase program of quality logs.

Jamestown Veneer and Plywood Company

The Jamestown Veneer and Plywood Company have had a mill at Poland, New York, since 1925 producing choice veneer from Adirondack logs.

The trend in log procurement has been away from company operations to contract operations and purchase logs.

Brant Excelsior

The Brant Excelsior mill on the Black River near Boonville has been operating since 1900. Walter Brant owned this mill for many years but sold it in 1951 to Stanley Presta who is the present owner.

This mill operates largely on aspen (popple) bolts and is supplied from the general area of the mill. Company operations, contract operations and purchase wood have been the method of procurement, with recent emphasis on purchase wood.

Willard Hazelton Operations

Willard Hazelton of Wilmington, New York, began in the lumber business in 1901 and has carried on a continuous operation since that time, largely in pine. In the earlier years, he carried on his own logging operations, in part, from company lands but is now depending more largely on contract and purchase logs. His sons have joined him in the operation.

A. O. Denton

A. O. Denton, who started in the lumber business near Elizabethtown, New York, about 1935, supplies part of his logs from his own operations on company lands.

Dorr Martin

Dorr T. Martin moved his lumbering operations from Steuben County in New York State to Lake George, New York, many years ago and has been operating in the Lake George area since that time. His log supply began on his own operations but is now supplied largely by contract and purchase logs. His son, David, has joined him in the operations and has now completed the construction of a large, modern mill in the Lake George site.

The J and C Lumber Company

The J and C Lumber Company, which is composed of Joseph and Chester Kwasniewski of West Leyden, New York, operated for several years in the Tug Hill and Moose River areas, largely on lands of the Gould Paper Company. They have more recently built a modern sawmill on the West Leyden-Osceola Road where they are carrying on an active program in Tug Hill hardwood.

Hayes Booher

Hayes Booher spent his early life in the Adirondacks where he served as a lumberjack and a logging operator. Much of his work was done for Clayton Elliott, who was the founder of the Elliott Hardwood Company. Mr. Booher later established the Booher Lumber Company and built a mill at Nedrow which is on the edge of Syracuse, New York. His son, Robert, later became president of the company.

Henry Helterline

Henry Helterline and son, Raymond, operated a mill at Stratford, New York, and lumber camps in the neighboring area for many years. They often entertained sky pilot Clarence Mason during his travels in the camps.

The sky pilot went about visiting these company operations in 1938. Some of them, such as the Gould Paper Company operations, were in familiar territory. Some others were in territory with which he had not been familiar. He soon became acquainted, however, with both the territory and the men.

LOGGING CONTRACTORS

The John E. Johnston Logging Operations

The Adirondack area also had a number of large and important logging and pulpwood contractors who normally operated several camps and employed a few hundred men. They might carry on operations for two or more companies at the same time.

John E. Johnston had several large operations under way when the writer returned as Adirondack sky pilot in 1938. Three of them were in Vermont.

In Vermont

William Mealus, who served for many years in the Moose River area, was superintendent of a large operation for Mr. Johnston above East Arlington on the Stratton Mountain country. "Chick" Ploof of St. Regis Falls, New York, and George Hayes, who had been a potato farmer in Aroostook County in Maine, were among the foremen. Martin Cummings served as the cook in one camp and Warren Howe in another while Mr. and Mrs. Brown of Port Leyden cooked at headquarters.

Mr. Johnston was getting out pulpwood which was trucked during the winter season to the International Paper Company mill at Corinth and the West Virginia Pulp & Paper Company mill at Mechanicville. The road in that area was a busy throughfare during the winter hauling season.

The Bellows Falls Ice Company cut the hardwood in the area and used Mr. Johnston's roads for their hauling operation. They had their crew housed in a small temporary village near Mr. Johnston's headquarters camp.

One man in the Bellows Falls crew had a small son who seemed to have an incurable disease. Dr. Nathaniel Norton, who was on the hospital staff at the Columbia Medical Center in New York City and spent his summers at Old Forge, New York, arranged for the boy to be examined and treated at the hospital, where he could have the best doctors in the country. Men in the John E. Johnston camps nearby furnished funds for the expenses of the boy and his father in New York. Hospital and medical services were furnished free of charge and the sky pilot took both the father and son to the hospital in New York City.

After a two-day stay in the city, the doctor, who was chief of the hospital staff, told the sky pilot, "we want him to stay about three days more to complete the diagnosis but it seems to be muscular dystrophy. If our diagnosis is correct, there is no known cure in the world today for the disease. We are carrying on extensive research to find a cure and hope we may find one soon." The diagnosis proved to be correct. The services of the country's outstanding doctors and the facilities of one of the nation's great hospitals had been put at the disposal of the boy from Stratton Mountain but there was no known cure.

Headquarters camp was near a monument along the road which marked the spot where Daniel Webster addressed the Whig Convention of 1840 with 15,000 in attendance. It was then a populated farming country, but farmers have been moving away from the region ever since as indicated by large trees growing in old cellars.

Clyde Kelly of St. Regis Falls, New York, was superintendent of an operation for Mr. Johnston on Dorset Mountain near Dorset, Vermont. The mountain was so steep that Clyde was hauling in the autumn season on dry ground with tractors. Winter hauling with snow or ice would have been impossible. During the previous year, Clyde had built a slide to get the pulpwood down the mountain, but the very steep slopes made even the slide ineffective. Blocks travelled at such a high rate of speed that control was impossible. The steep mountain operation made a very good setting for moving pictures.

Patrick Chiasson was superintendent of an operation for Mr. Johnston on a mountain southwest of West Rutland, Vermont, and made his home in West Rutland. Joe LaRue was foreman in one camp.

The sky pilot spent an interesting evening in late fall with the West Rutland crew and a comfortable night at camp. After an early breakfast he made the drive down the dirt road a few miles to the main highway. It was about daylight and a fall of fresh snow during the night made the road quite slippery in case of a sudden change of speed or direction. As he approached a bridge, which was on a curve of the road, a truck appeared ahead travelling at a good rate of speed. The only solution seemed to be a head-on collision with the truck, as the brakes were not effective on the slippery snow. The truck, however, was driven by a fast thinking truck driver with quick reflexes. He pulled his truck into an open gate on the roadside and the sky pilot stopped behind the truck. There was no collision or damage. The truck driver said, "I didn't expect to meet anyone on this road at this hour and was boiling right along." His fast thinking and quick reflexes had avoided an accident which probably would have eliminated the Adirondack sky pilot.

At Jerseyfield Lake

As World War II approached and the demand for pulpwood increased greatly, Mr. Johnston opened several other operations. One of these was at Jerseyfield Lake north of Dolgeville, New York, where Dewitt Wiley supervised the cutting of a large virgin tract for the West Virginia Pulp and Paper Company. There were several camps on this operation. The largest pine cut on this tract was 52 inches in diameter while the largest spruce was 48 inches.

The sky pilot observed several new developments on this operation including: the first chain saw in use in the Adirondacks (of German make); the first bulldozer in operation on log road construction; a slide used to horse haul logs from one lake to another by chaining several logs end-to-end and a loader used in loading large four-foot blocks. The log hauling season on the Jerseyfield tract was a period when a log truck went past headquarters camp every few minutes from early morning until late evening. Oftentimes one truck was immediately behind the other.

On the Jessup River

With the completion of the operations in Vermont, John E. Johnston moved his logging and camp equipment and crews to a large operation on lands of the International Paper Company north of Speculator and set up headquarters at Perkins Clearing. William Mealus was superintendent of this operation until his retirement when he was succeeded by Clyde Kelley.

Mr. Johnston had several camps on this operation run by "Chick" Ploof, Fred Poulin, William Bouchard, John Farrell and Charles Tate as foremen. Wood from this operation was landed on the Jessup River for driving to Indian Lake. It was trucked from the Indian Lake jack works to the mill at Corinth, New York. Horses were used extensively on both the skidding and hauling operations but tractor use was on the increase.

The major inovation in the Speculator job was the extensive use of the chain saw on the landing at one of the camps. One two-man chain saw crew cut seven thousand cords from sixteen-foot logs into four-foot pulp, and dropped it into a conveyor which conveyed it out into the stream. This landing operation laid the foundation for expansion of chain saw use in the Adirondacks. Mr. Johnston trained his chain saw operator as a mechanic and set up a shop on the Cedar River next season to service forty chain saws used in two camps. Mr. Johnston saw that service was the clue to chain saw use and eliminated that bottleneck immediately.

One afternoon in the early winter of 1943, the sky pilot started out from Perkins Clearing headquarters for a ten-mile hike back to one of the camps. As the time was 4:30, he expected to make camp at 7:30 in time to conduct a service in the bunkhouse. He had a pack on his back with some magazines, some New Testament gospels, shaving articles, a flashlight and extra batteries.

The trip went along on schedule for the first five miles. The flashlight illuminated the road after darkness came on about 5:30. Suddenly the flashlight went out and the trial of new batteries indicated that the bulb had blown out, with no replacement. The night was dark in the woods so one couldn't see the toteroad, and it was snowing a little. The sky pilot discovered that the only way of guidance on the road was to keep one foot always in the sleigh runner track and turn when the track turned. The rest of the journey was made by that method but progress was slow. At a point where the log road crossed the toteroad the situation was a bit confusing but matches and a newspaper furnished light for that emergency.

At last, the sky pilot climbed a familiar hill and there before him lay the camp a short distance away with lights somewhat dim. The time, however, was not 7:30 p.m. but 10 p.m. Following the toteroad in the dark had been a slow and tedious process. He reached camp, found a vacant bed in the office and retired somewhat exhausted and hungry but was soon fast asleep. A peaceful night's sleep eliminated the exhaustion and a lumber camp breakfast the hunger, but the memory of that evening hike remains as vivid as ever.

The City of Nobleboro

With the conclusion of their contract for Gould Paper Company on Tug Hill, Elmer Bernier and Mr. Johnston moved their equipment to Nobleboro on West Canada Creek where they made a large cut of rough four-foot pulpwood for the J. P. Lewis Company of Beaver Falls, New York, and the St. Regis Paper Company mill at Deferiet, New York.

The cut which involved the operation of several camps on the West Canada and Jones Brook, continued over several years.

The handling of this big supply of pulpwood required the construction of a large dam on the West Canada at Nobleboro where the rough pulpwood was debarked in a barking drum and loaded on trucks for shipment. The construction of the dam and the spring drives were conducted under the supervision of Joe Morin who had also been Elmer Bernier's right hand man on Tug Hill. Joe died suddenly at camp near the end of the Nobleboro operation.

Nobleboro was a busy place during the logging activities on the West Canada and was commonly called "The City of Nobleboro."

CLARENCE J. STRIFE

Clarence J. Strife was born and reared at Jerden Falls near Carthage, New York, where he combined an operation in hemlock bark for the neighboring tannery with work on his father's farm. He devoted his life to logging and was a partner of John E. Johnston in the Little Rapids Lumber Company at Brandreth, New York.

The Big Depression deprived Mr. Strife of his fortune as it did many people. In 1938 he was beginning a comeback with headquarters at Old Forge and a log job on lands of the Adirondack League Club just south of Old Forge.

Mr. Strife expanded his operations the next year with three camps on the Adirondack League Club, one camp on the International Paper Company lands near the Beaver River and one job at Brandreth. Joseph Lindsay of Old Forge was Mr. Strife's head clerk at the Old Forge

93

office, with Oral Wolfe handling clerical duties in the woods. Frank Dakir, Robert Higman and Ed Smith were foreman in the camps.

Clarence Strife was in process of becoming one of the largest logging operators in Northern New York with camps in several parts of the Adirondacks and on Tug Hill. He was using the obstacles of the Big Depression as stepping stones to greater achievements and more useful living. He had only limited educational opportunities as a boy but attained such a high degree of knowledge of the forest and logging methods that his advice was sought by many company executives and foresters throughout Northern New York.

SISSON AND WHITE

Sisson and White was a logging and pulpwood operating partnership composed of Stanley Sisson and Donald White, both of Potsdam, New York. Stanley was the son of George Sisson who was President of the Raquette River Paper Company. Donald White was George Sisson's son-in-law.

These operators had two camps making a large pulpwood cut at the Usher Farm back of Childwold, New York. Jerry Hayes and James Sullivan of South Colton, New York, were the experienced foremen in these camps. Next year they moved to a large operation at Seveys which is along the Raquette River below Tupper Lake.

Stanley Sisson had some additional operations of his own, including one on lands of the International Paper Company near Childwold. This job was run by John Davignon of Tupper Lake who was also one of the Adirondack's largest logging operators.

Stanley was also cutting on Whitney Park near Long Lake and had Arthur LaPorte of Tupper Lake as one operator in this area. Arthur, like John Davignon, had spent his life in logging.

One day in late summer the sky pilot visited one of the Sisson and White camps and was a little late for the evening meal which included green corn on the cob. As one man completed his meal, he said, "I guess thirteen ears will be enough for tonight."

After the man had left the cook camp, the sky pilot inquired of the cook whether this statement was a joke. The cook replied "Oh no, he ate thirteen ears of corn along with other things for supper. He is a bucksaw man and cuts eight cords or more per day which takes a lot of energy. He takes two pounds of meat and a good quantity of bread, vegetables, coffee and pie out to the woods each morning for his lunch." It was little wonder that the camp cooks were busy men preparing meals for rugged workmen.

Ernest and Wilfred Dechene of Tupper Lake, New York, had their early training on log jobs around Carter, New York, where their father was a logging and pulpwood operator. They later carried on operations in cooperation with Clarence Strife of Old Forge. Ernest operated largely in the Tupper Lake area while Wilfred had an extensive program for Donald Rice on the South Branch of the Moose River.

Adirondack Colleges

The Adirondack area had two very good forestry colleges which trained men for various capacities in forestry.

The New York State Ranger School at Wanakena was established in 1912 and operates as part of the State University College of Forestry at Syracuse. It has a one year forestry training program which receives full credit for one year's work at a university or prepares men for forestry work in the field.

Prof. James Dubuar began his service as director at the Ranger School in 1919 and continued in that capacity for thirty-eight years. He is recognized throughout the nation for his outstanding service in forestry education. Prof. Lucien Plumley succeeded Mr. Dubuar as director of the ranger school.

Upon his death, in 1937, Phelps Smith left his estate for the establishment of a college which was chartered in 1937 as Paul Smith's College with courses in forestry, hotel management and liberal arts.

Dr. Chester L. Buxton came as the President of the college in 1948 and has continued in that capacity. Under his leadership, many new buildings have been added to the campus. Student enrollment has grown from 150 to 900.

William Rutherford was called from the U. S. Forest Service in 1950 to become the head of the forestry department. This department has grown steadily in enrollment and in quality of teaching program. Its graduates are in demand both in forest industries and public forestry.

Flying to Lumber Camps

The sky pilot experimented with a new method of transportation to lumber camps as the logging program progressed. His son Elwyn was flying a seaplane in the Adirondacks for two summers. Why not use the plane for transportation to some of the camps? Use it he did on several occasions where the camp was near to a lake. The arrival of the plane was always greeted with keen interest by members of the crew. The men were ordinarily all down at the water's edge to observe the departure. A trip to a camp in any part of the Adirondacks could be made in a short time.

The plane was useful also for filming pictures, especially in the autumn season when colors were brilliant. This program enabled the sky pilot to build up a movie film of autumn scenes which are of indescribable beauty.

On a flight from the Cedar River camp one clear evening, Elwyn climbed to an altitude of five thousand feet from which one could get a birdseye view of the entire Adirondacks stretching from Whiteface Mountain on the north to the Mohawk Valley, and from Tug Hill on the west to the Green Mountains of Vermont. This was the writer's most spectacular view in a lifetime.

The sky pilot left the Adirondack Lumber Camp Parish in 1949 to return for a five-year pastorate at Niccolls Memorial Church in Old Forge and Big Moose Community Chapel. He was succeeded in the camps for a while by Elmer Jennsen of Michigan. A back injury caused Mr. Jennsen to leave the parish and return to a church in Saginaw, Michigan.

Work on the expanded "Lumber Camp News" and the Woodsmen's Club was continued during the Old Forge pastorate of the writer. His daughter, Winifred, served as Director of Religious Education in the Old Forge-Big Moose parish.

Major projects at the parish in Old Forge during that period included a vigorous youth group from the entire Central Adirondack area in the summer and a group of ten students from Union Seminary who combined forest salvage work after the 1950 blowdown with work in several rural parishes including the one at Old Forge. A major event also was the ordination of the pastor's son, Ralph, in the Old Forge church and his call to a pastorate in Troy, Pennsylvania. He is now serving in Leopoldville in the Congo.

THE WOODSMEN'S CLUB

As the sky pilot went about his work among the Adirondack and Tug Hill lumber camps, it was evident that there were some sources of strength and sources of weakness in the program. There was little doubt about the reactions and interest of the men. They were friendly on camp visits and attentive at the services in the bunkhouses. They were appreciative of the efforts of one who understood their interests and problems and adapted himself to the way of life in the lumber camps which were their real home.

The major problem for these men arose on their occasional trips to the village or city where they were a commercial opportunity. They were strong and hardworking men who were dedicated to their work but had never learned to play. The people outside were anxious to help them in the play process for a sufficient price. Some of them were married men who supported their families well and went home on their trips outside. Some others also saved their money and spent it wisely on their trips. The majority however, spent their hard-earned wages quite unwisely. Alcohol was their major problem on these journeys. What could be done about it?

It seemed evident that a clubhouse in whose ownership and operation the old-time lumberjack would share with his fellow workmen might offer at least a partial solution. Such a clubhouse should provide comfortable beds, good meals, showers and some recreation facilities.

This possibility was discussed at services in the camps and men expressed favorable reaction. After some discussion, the crew at Clarence Strife's camp near Bisby Lake signed up as members in the early summer of 1942. Crews in other camps followed with similar action until Club membership reached a figure of about 600.

Purchase of a Club House

In the meantime, possible sites were investigated. A large double house in the village of Forestport became available for $2,250. It was purchased later that summer and a substantial down payment made. Plans were made for improvements to the building and the addition of furniture.

Thomas Peckham, who was cook at Ed Smith's camp near Saranac Lake, suggested a place where beds could be purchased at a reasonable price. Twenty beds were purchased and delivered to the clubhouse by truck. Elwyn, Ralph and Fred Reed spent their Christmas vacation sanding and painting the beds until they looked new. The Boonville American Legion and some communities and churches decided to repair and furnish rooms. The interior of the building was completely repaired, including papering, painting and necessary fixtures.

Twenty mattresses, which had been marked down at a sale, were purchased from a wholesale store in Albany. Surplus blankets became available from the National Lead Company at Tahawus at factory price. Hotel dishes were purchased from Becker's Hotel near Old Forge. The Forestport and Woodgate people participated actively in papering, painting and furnishing rooms. This group included Miss Nettie Bentliff, Mrs. Lulu Chandler, Henry Rubyor, Mrs. Carolyn Hopkins, Mrs. Harriet Lyon, Mrs. Eliza Scanlon, Curtis Smith, Howard Smith, and Ed Raymond.

Plans were made to open the clubhouse on March 11, 1943, which was the seventy-fifth birthday of Rev. C. W. Mason, and all worked to have the Club ready at that time. It did open on that date with a fine dinner which was prepared by camp cook, Sam LeMay from the Finch Pruyn and Company camps at Newcomb, with the cooperation of Mrs. Harriett Lyon and other ladies from Forestport. The seventy-five people in attendance filled the living room and office as well as the dining room. Clarence Mason and Aaron Maddox were present to share in the occasion and made short speeches. Dr. Howard Yargin, who had succeeded Dr. U. L. Mackey as Synodical Superintendent, also took part.

The clubhouse was ready for occupancy as well as for the dinner. It had twelve rooms, seven of which were equipped with twenty comfortable beds. Two living rooms were furnished with rugs, easy chairs and tables for cards and other games. The office had some comfortable chairs along with a supply of soft drinks, tobacco, cigarettes, candy and a telephone. The dining room had places for thirty-five men with a well equipped kitchen to supply the food. Showers upstairs and down provided ample opportunity for cleanliness. Camp cook Sam LeMay was there to supply the food and care for the clubhouse.

The Lumberjack in His New Home

Several men took advantage of the facilities of the clubhouse during the spring vacation season. Some of them stayed for the period of their spring vacations and found that they could have a vacation of several weeks for one hundred dollars. Most of those who stayed at the club came sober and remained sober for the period of their stay. A little later in the spring season, a few, who had already had a more hilarious time in the city, came and had to be put to bed. The management reminded them that the drinking program was not to be continued at the club and most of them cooperated.

Later in the spring, Sam LeMay returned to spend some time with his family in the Province of Quebec, and Mrs. Carolyn Hopkins of Woodgate took over the management of the club with some help from her son, Gordon, and Ralph and Fred Reed. Mrs. Harriett Lyon and her daughter, Loretta, cooperated also on special occasions.

Both meat and gasoline were scarce in that period which made it necessary to devise ways of meeting the scarcity. A flock of two hundred chickens in the club henhouse provided both eggs and chickens for the table. Seven young pigs grew into good sized hogs and enriched the table. Bushels of fruit were picked and frozen at the Boonville Frozen Food Locker for winter and spring use. A good sized garden at the clubhouse supplied vegetables and a field of potatoes provided that part of daily needs. A pickup truck made out of a $75 second-hand car provided the necessary transportation of supplies. Gordon Hopkins and the Reed boys did most of the necessary work on these projects such as the garden, potatoes, fruit and the flock of chickens while they were attending school at Forestport. They had a summer assist from James Hill, who was a young ministerial student serving the Forestport church for the summer.

The "Lumber Camp News" office was also housed at the Woodsmen's Club where Mrs. Hilda Avery and Ralph Reed did the secretarial work. Mrs. Hopkins also rendered valuable service in securing advertising in Boonville, Tupper Lake, northern New England, and other places.

Several men made their homes at the club during the vacation season for the period of its operation in Forestport 1943-1948. This group included Joe Anderson, Joe Capioca, Frank Caster, Stuart Jackson, Louis Maski, Jack Moore, Clem Stachek and others. Most of these men served as Directors of the Club. All of these men have since passed away.

The operation of the Clubhouse at Forestport gave the sky pilot an opportunity for closer contact with the men during their vacation periods in the spring and at Christmas time, when logging in the woods had come to a halt because of muddy conditions. This association included occasional card games and many interesting visits around the table or in the living room in the evening.

Big, Big John, who was the biggest man working in the Adirondack camps, came to the club for a few days on occasion. He had grown up in the Ukraine but left there during the period of the Bolshevik Revolution and came to the Adirondacks. John was violently opposed to Communism and was always suspicious of spies in the country. He had a tendency toward a nervous condition which was increased by his fear of spy operations.

The sky pilot's major effort to help John under these conditions was to listen to the story of his experiences, suspicions and fears often until late in the evening. This acted as a sort of safety valve which relieved the nervous pressure for a few weeks.

Louis was also a big man who had come from Poland in the period of the Russian revolution. He worked with a crew of tree surgeons for a time but later went to the Adirondack lumber camps where he rendered great service in felling, skidding, bucking and hauling of logs and pulpwood. His size and strength were supplemented by great skill and an intelligent approach to his daily toil.

Louis had come to America alone and had no family. He enjoyed his work and life in the camps where he was perfectly at home. Like many other lumberjacks, however, Louis had never learned to play. His

99

occasional trips to the city were spent in drinking and he returned to the woods each time to replace "the stake" which he had lost so quickly in the barroom.

When Louis came to the Club, he decided to go on the water wagon and did just that. He opened a bank account and saved the surplus money which he brought out on his trips to the Club. In two years he had sufficient funds to purchase a truck on a cash basis and went in business for himself with the truck. This made a fine occupation for a man who had served effectively for years in the woods but was now ready for semi-retirement.

"John the Baptist" came from a rural community in West Virginia where he combined work in the woods with that of a local preacher. The death of his wife led him to travel north where he worked in the Adirondack lumber camps. Sorrow led him to alcohol as it has many other people.

John and the sky pilot had many interesting visits in the bunkhouses at camp and at the Woodsmen's Club on one occasion. John decided to give up drinking completely as the way to victory over appetite. He rendered distinguished service in the woods for some years and then moved to Boonville, New York, where he served as policeman at the school. John took great delight in guiding the small children across the busy street to places of safety. The children were equally fond of him.

A Doctor Returns to His Practice

One day the sky pilot was washing the car in his driveway at Old Forge, when a tall man stopped his car and approached. As he extended his hand, he said, "I am Dr. John Doe from the medical staff of X University. You don't know me but I have seen you several times. I was an alcoholic and left the staff of the medical school to work in the Adirondack lumber camps. I have been present several times in lumber camps where you have conducted services and have stayed occasionally at the Woodsmen's Club in Forestport. Now I just stopped to tell you that I have found the way to victory and am back on the staff of the medical school again." This was a striking illustration of the fact that "God moves in mysterious ways His wonders to perform."

Some have described the old-time lumberjack as one who was prone to fight. The writer's observations and experiences have been quite the opposite. Lumberjacks got along well together in the camps. The sky pilot spent several thousand evenings in bunkhouses and never saw a fight. There was seldom an argument. These men spent their energies in long hours of labor and useful effort. Why would they argue and fight?

100

One exception to this was a quarrelsome man by the name of Tommy who stayed for a while at the Club. One day he said he was going to slap the sky pilot and squared around to do so. Just then he "hit the deck" on the clubhouse floor and regained consciousness a while later. This was the only time the sky pilot had to use physical force with an old-time lumberjack to maintain order at the Club.

The Burial of Old-Time Lumberjacks

In the summer of 1942 a new problem arose. Phil Souci, who was a skilled old-time lumberjack and river driver as well as a member of the Club, died in Utica without known relatives in the United States. Where should he be buried and who would make arrangements? The answer to this question came in the purchase of a plot in Beechwood Cemetery at Forestport with room for thirty graves. The Club made the funeral arrangements and the sky pilot conducted the funeral service with several of Phil's old friends present. Most of those present have since been laid at rest beside him in Beechwood Cemetery.

This action on Phil's burial place led to the purchase of plots in other cemeteries at Boonville, Old Forge, Tupper Lake and Wells and the ultimate placing of monuments including the names of men with this inscription: "Dedicated in memory of men who have rendered distinguished service to their fellowmen and their country in Adirondack lumber camps."

The Club Buys a New Home

In the summer of 1947, Charles Law, who was then woodlands manager for the Gould Paper Company, visited the clubhouse and brought some maps along indicating the location of logging operations for the next ten years. He advised moving the club to Old Forge which would be nearer the center of operations. The Club Directors considered the question carefully and investigated possible sites. They decided to sell the Forestport Clubhouse to Raymond Dufresne, who was a logging operator living at Forestport, and to purchase the schoolhouse at Thendara, which is adjacent to Old Forge. They decided also to ask several Adirondack forest industries to cooperate in the program and to furnish part of the Board of Directors. James E. Davis, who had succeeded Charles Law as woodlands manager of the Gould Paper Company; Clarence Strife; Louis Seheult of Finch Pruyn and Company, and Roy Lavoy of the Oval Wood Dish Company, became active members of the Board of Directors. These and other companies gave substantial amounts to purchase the

Thendara school. Equipment was moved from the Forestport Club and the balance left over from the sale of the building was applied to the purchase of the new clubhouse.

The Thendara school was a four-room building with two furnaces, one of which was used to heat each side. Stokers were added to the furnaces and a carload of coal put in the coalbin. The school room upstairs on one side was partitioned off to provide sleeping rooms and the room underneath was partitioned for kitchen, dining room and a room for the cook. The second room upstairs was set up with several beds in dormitory style and the room underneath was furnished as a large living room which could serve also as a dining room for banquets. The clubhouse at Thendara opened with the 6th Annual Woodsmen's Club Dinner which was held at the clubhouse in March, 1948. The Annual Woodsmen's Dinner has since been held at the Fire Hall or the Masonic Club rooms at Old Forge, and in Tupper Lake.

The Thendara clubhouse was open for the entertainment of men for the spring of 1948 and five seasons after that. Martin Cummings and Mrs. Belle Burnett, of West Leyden, took turns as cook most of the period and others served for short seasons. The clubhouse was also used for "The Northern Logger" office for three summer seasons.

In the period of World War II, Prof. A. B. Recknagel was called from his duties at Cornell University to stimulate increased pulpwood production in the nation. He ran a series of bucksaw contests in Northern New York to help achieve that goal. One of these contests near the Woodsmen's Club at Thendara attracted a group of a few hundred who watched Leland and Donald Marcellus from Schaghticoke, New York, win the bucksaw contest. This gave the club directors the idea that chopping and sawing contests might be of interest. They decided to run such a contest in the summer of 1948 as an experiment.

The Woodsmen's Field Days

The committee which planned this first Woodsmen's Field Day at Old Forge was composed of: Louis Seheult of Finch Pruyn and Company, chairman; James E. Davis of the Gould Paper Company, Roy Lavoy of the Oval Wood Dish Corporation, Clarence J. Strife of Old Forge and Frank Reed. The field day attracted about 1,300 people who sat on a hillside to observe the events at the foot of the small hill. The committee unexpectedly concluded the event with a $600 balance which was used on the Woodsmen's Club program. Plans were made for another in Tupper Lake in 1949. That attracted about 6,000 people. The Field Day was held in Tupper Lake from 1949 to 1962 and in Boonville 1962-1963. It is now alternating between Boonville and Tupper Lake.

Several of the foresters and forest industry men in the Tupper Lake area furnished active leadership in the Woodsmen's Field Day and some of them became Directors of the Woodsmen's Club. The list included Gardner Blake of U. S. Bobbin, Frank Bencze of the Oval Wood Dish Corp., John Curry of U. S. Forest Service, logging operators Ernest and Wilfred Dechene; trucking operator Vincent Kavanagh; Orrin Latham of the Ranger School; Robert O'Neal of Elliott Hardwood Co.; Sam Parmelee and Oscar Ohman of the Draper Corp.; District Forester William Petty; William Rutherford and Gould Hoyt of Paul Smith's College; David Short of Whitney Industries, and John Stock, who later became general superintendent for Litchfield Industries.

The Woodsmen's Field Day at Boonville also produced several outstanding leaders. These included Livingston Lansing, Richard Ferris, John Mahaffy, Leon Renodin, Newell Wagner, Paul Woolschlager of the local community; Tony Lado of Pettibone Mulliken at Rome; Robert Bramhall of the J. P. Lewis Co.; Kelly Dickinson of Diamond National; Duane Irwin of Northern Lumber Company, and Mr. and Mrs. Joseph Kwasniewski of the J and C. Lumber Company.

State Forester Perry Merrill of Vermont studied the field day program in 1951 and started a similar event at Lake Dunmore near Brandon in 1952. It has run successfully since that time, largely under the leadership of Assistant State Forester Art Heitman.

James Elliott of Coudersport, Pennsylvania, studied the program also in 1951 and started a similar program at Cherry Springs Park near Galeton and Coudersport in 1952. This has been operating with growing interest since that time under the sponsorship of the Penn-York Lumbermen's Club with Ben F. Kramer of Galeton as chairman.

Sam Hall of the Draper Corporation, Henry Waldo of Franconia Paper Company and County Forester Leslie Sargent of Lincoln, New Hampshire, have run a woodsmen's Field Day at the Plymouth Fair in Plymouth for the last few years. Ivan Owens of the Packaging Corporation of America started the very successful Great Lakes Forestry Exposition at Mio., Michigan. Some help was also extended to the Berlin Fair in Berlin, Connecticut, for such a show. One has run for the last few years in Rhode Island. Maine took up the idea with shows at Ashland and Carabassett in the summer of 1964. In each case, information has been requested and supplied from the office at Old Forge.

The success of the logging shows in several states led to plans for a Northeastern Lumberjack Championship in 1956 as part of the program

103

of the Northeastern Loggers' Association. This has brought together the state champions in eight states for exciting contests to determine the Northeastern champions in chopping, sawing and log rolling.

Walter Adams of Hoosick Falls, New York; David Geer of Jewett City, Connecticut; Sven Johnson of Voluntown, Connecticut and Arden Cogar of Webster Springs, West Virginia have been chopping champions. William Johnston and William Rope of Australia also gave outstanding demonstrations of great skill and speed in the use of the axe.

John and Edward Kocjancic of Johnsonburg and Kane, Pennsylvania have been consistent winners in the crosscut sawing contests.

The list of chairmen for the Northeastern Championship includes Siegfried Tolle of Pownal, Vermont; John Hovak of Broadalbin, New York; Frank Bencze of Tupper Lake, New York and Robert Bramhall of Beaver Falls, New York.

The Adirondack Lumbermen's Association

In the early 1950's Adirondack sawmill operators felt the need for an organization and formed the Adirondack Lumbermen's Association. Nelson Nash of The Great Eastern Lumber Company at North Creek led the organization movement.

The leadership of the Association has included Stuart Carpenter of Carpenter and Sunderland at Broadalbin, Edward Orwig of the Penn-York Lumber Corporation at Fort Edward, Joseph Collins of the Murphy Lumber Company at Chestertown, Al Blakely of Broadalbin, Thomas McPhillips of McPhillips Brothers at The Glen, Robert Sweet and Everett Frulla of Warrensburg, Maurice Frulla of Indian Lake, Charles Hazelton of the Hazelton Lumber Company of Wilmington, Stewart Irwin and Kenneth Trushaw of the Northern Lumber Company at Poland.

Major projects of the Association have been providing a Christmas tree for the White House lawn in Washington, D. C., and cooperation with *The Northern Logger* and Woodsmen's Club in an effective program of promotion in the use of beech.

The Association program centers largely in the Warrensburg area where several of the Adirondack mills are located.

GROWTH OF "THE LUMBER CAMP NEWS"

"When you go to Maine, look up William Hilton of the Great Northern Paper Company." This statement was made to the sky pilot one day early in the 1940's by an old time lumberjack in one of the Finch Pruyn camps at Newcomb, New York.

A short time later he did go to Maine and looked up William Hilton who was woodlands manager of the Great Northern Paper Company with headquarters at Bangor. Mr. Hilton proved to be a splendid host and became a good friend. He wrote out information on Great Northern's pulpwood operations and looked up material, including pictures, for an illustrated story.

On a trip to Bangor a few months later, the editor had a damaged tire at a time when tires, as well as gas, were rationed and were difficult to get. He asked Mr. Hilton's suggestions on a spare tire for his journey in Maine and the return trip home. Mr. Hilton pointed out of the office window and remarked, "Do you see that building over on the hill? Go over and tell Joe that William Hilton sent you. Joe will fix you up." Joe did just that. He provided a tire which ran for several thousand miles.

A Good Reception in Maine

The friendliness and cooperation of William Hilton were indicative of the spirit which the writer found among other woodlands managers of paper companies. These included James E. Davis of Maine Seaboard at Buckport, Robert Drummond and Harry Beach of Oxford Paper Company at Rumford, William Eggleston of Eastern Corporation at Brewer, Louis Freedman of the Penobscot Purchasing Company at Great Works, R. E. Hendricks of the International Paper Company at Livermore Falls, Edward Melcher of the S. D. Warren Company at Cumberland Mills, Frank Pearson of the Eastern Pulpwood Company at Calais, O. A. Sawyer of Hollingsworth and Whitney at Waterville, and others. C. S. Herr of Brown Company at Berlin, Lester Fogg of Groveton Paper Company and Henry Waldo of Parker-Young at Lincoln were New Hampshire men who were also very friendly and cooperative. Henry had succeeded Sherm Adams in the position at Parker-Young a short time before. Robert Monahan of Dartmouth College also helped enthusiastically on the program.

Forest Commissioner Al Nutting and his associate, Austin Wilkins, cooperated actively in supplying information, articles and photographs which helped readers of the "Lumber Camp News" to become familiar with the vast forest resources of Maine and the problems involved in their protection and management.

Robert Ashman, who was Director of the Forestry Department at the University of Maine, and Professor Henry Plummer of his faculty also took an active part in developing the service of the "Lumber Camp News"

105

in the state. Henry Plummer was a former resident of Boonville, New York, where the publication was printed and was familiar with both its program and opportunities of growth.

Several sawmill operators and other forest industries also were very hospitable and cooperative in furnishing information for the columns of the "Lumber Camp News." These included Phil Chadbourne of Bethel, James Flagg of Naples, R. D. Hinckley of Ellsworth, Thomas Hammond of East Hiram, C. B. Cummings of Norway, Rand Stowell of Dixfield, Saunders Brothers of Westbrook, Joe Wilner of Norway, Leon Williams of East Eddington, and many others.

Manufacturers of logging equipment in Northern New England cooperated actively in the advertising program which helped to develop the "Lumber Camp News" in volume and news coverage as well as circulation.

Wayne Lewison, who was manager of the Bobbin Division of Draper Corporation at Beebe River, New Hampshire, proved to be a splendid host and a real friend. Wayne was a graduate of Iowa State University and was engaged in building up the Bobbin Division as well as a sound forestry program for the company. He was opening operations also in Maine, Vermont and New York State to supply bobbin blanks for the finishing plant at Beebe River. The New York State project at Tupper Lake, under the management of Sam Parmelee, has been a permanent part of the company's program along with the Beebe River operation. The purchase of a large tract of land in the northern Adirondacks in 1945 and the construction of a new mill at Tupper Lake in 1948 were important steps in the development program. Wayne was destined to play an important role in developing the "Lumber Camp News" service.

Expansion in Southern New York

The sky pilot extended his editorial program to his old home country in southern New York and called on several men who were operating mills, particularly in hardwood. These mills were located in country where the virgin pine and hemlock had been cut at an earlier time.

These calls included Howard Hanlon of Cotton-Hanlon at Odessa, George Burd of Canisteo, Courtney Norton at Little Valley, Tadder Brothers at Avoca, the Slawson Lumber Company of Hunt, Carl Sirianni of Greene, and other sawmill operators.

On the call to the Norton mill at Little Valley, Courtney Norton took the writer for a ride through his large forest in the jeep. He took real pride in his fine stands of maple, oak, pine and other species. As he concluded the journey through the forest, Mr. Norton remarked, "I am the fourth generation on this farm and woodlot. I want to pass it on to my sons better than I found it."

Courtney Norton died a few months after this trip and did pass his farm and forest on to his sons better than he found it. Upon the occasion of his death, the writer found that he was a member of the school board, an active officer in the church and a leader in the Boy Scout movement. He had a deep sense of spiritual values, of which the stewardship of the forest was an important part.

The sky pilot became well acquainted with Howard Hanlon at Odessa on these trips and came to share the view of other lumbermen in the area that Howard Hanlon was one of the leading lumbermen of the Northeast and rated high among lumbermen in the nation. Like Courtney Norton, Howard has served on the school board for years, has been an active officer in the church and a leader in the Boy Scouts, as well as active in other important groups.

The development of the service of the "Lumber Camp News" over a much wider area including Northern New England and Southern New York helped to make it a much larger and somewhat more useful publication. It grew in size from four pages in 1939 to forty-eight pages and in circulation from three hundred to fifteen hundred.

Some trips also were taken from Southern New York into Pennsylvania to visit mills and forestry projects. These trips included calls on Lawrence Krimm at Williamsport, William Lynn of West Virginia Pulp and Paper at Tyrone, R. J. Gustafson of the Endeavor Lumber Company at Endeavor, William Young of Fisher and Young at Titusville and James Elliott, who had a mill at Coudersport. Both James Elliott and William Lynn took part in the development program as the "Lumber Camp News" became a magazine. Calls were made also at Penn State University and the Department of Forests and Waters, where Maurice Goddard, Ralph Bible, Joseph Ibberson and others gave valuable cooperation.

"Fun in the News"

The "Lumber Camp News" developed a "Fun In The News" section quite early in its program. This brought in some amusing stories from a wide variety of sources.

Story from Mountainous Area of the South

A man and his wife lived in a remote mountainous area where they had little contact with civilization outside. One day a traveller through the area gave the man a mirror.

107

The mountaineer remarked as he looked in the mirror, "My father's pitcher, I didn't know my father had his pitcher took." He didn't like the looks of the be-whiskered old cuss and hid the mirror in the attic.

The wife's curiosity about something which her husband had hid led her to a search in the attic, where she finally uncovered the mirror. She remarked as she took a look at it, "So that's the old hag he's been chasing."

Railroad Stories

A man climbed into a Pullman car in the Grand Central Station late one evening and said to the colored porter, "I have an important appointment in Syracuse in the morning. I am a hard man to awaken but am giving you this money. You see that I get off the train in Syracuse."

The passenger retired shortly afterwards and soon fell asleep. When he awakened and looked out the window, the sun was shining brightly. He called the same porter over and inquired, "Where are we now?"

The porter, "We will be in Buffalo in a few minutes."

This information made the passenger violently angry and he began to censure the porter in terms that were hardly fit for a Pullman car. When it had gone on for a few minutes the conductor called the porter over and said, "You are expected to be courteous to people on the train but don't have to stand language like that."

The porter replied, "If you think that's bad, you should have heard the man I put off in Syracuse."

A porter met a travelling man at the train and inquired, "Where are your bags?"

The traveller, "I don't have any bags."

The porter, "Aren't you a travelling man?"

The traveller, "Yes."

The porter, "What are you selling?"

The traveller, "Brains."

The porter, "You are the first travelling man I ever saw who didn't have any samples with him."

A Vermont Story

A new minister in a Vermont village attended the town meeting a few weeks after he arrived in town. They began the meeting with the election of important village officers and worked down the scale to the less important. They finally came to the office of hog constable.

A wit in the audience remarked, "I nominate the new minister for hog constable."

The minister (rising quickly), "I came here a few weeks ago thinking of my work as that of being a shepherd but you folks know better than I what my title should be."

Story from a Forestry College

Some foresters telegraphed the President of the college to send a good speaker for an important meeting and stated that they wanted a great wit.

The President telegraphed in return, "No great wit available. Am sending two half wits."

World War I Stories

A young man in Chicago enlisted in the army and went overseas but failed to write home. When there was no response from letters sent to him over a period of some months, the father thought of a novel way to get a response and sent this telegram, "Store on the North Side burned last night. Twenty-five thousand dollars insurance."

When there was no response after several weeks, he sent another telegram, "Store on the East Side burned last night. Fifty thousand dollars insurance."

In desperation after some more weeks, the father sent a third telegram, "Store on South Side burned last night. Seventy-five thousand dollars insurance."

This message brought a short response by telegraph, "Keep the home fires burning."

A new recruit went about the yard, the barracks and the parade ground picking up bits of paper wherever he saw one. Each time he would say, "That isn't it."

The company officers thought this strange habit indicated mental trouble on the part of the new recruit and sent him to the medical staff. After three examinations, the medical men decided that he was insane and recommended that he be discharged.

When the young man received his discharge he looked at it carefully for a time and then remarked, "That's it."

Miscellaneous

A group of ladies were at a card party when conversation turned to their husbands. One lady spoke of her husband in very complimentary terms. One of the other ladies inquired, "Does your husband smoke?" She replied, "My husband does like a good cigar after a real good dinner, but I don't think he smokes more than three or four cigars a year."

John: "A horse was on a high bank of a deep ravine through which a mountain stream flowed and there was a pile of hay and grain on the other side but no bridge over the stream. How did the horse get over to get the hay and grain?"

(A long pause on the part of Joe.)

John: "Do you give up?"

Joe: "Yes."

John: "So did the horse."

Back in 1940 the editor bruised his nose through contact with the door of a truck. The following evening he met a Dr. Louis of Vernon, New York.

The writer: "Dr. Louis, it seems to me I have met you before."

Dr. Louis: (looking at the editor's nose) "No. I think it was Joe Louis you met."

Dedicated People Insure Progress

The extension of "Lumber Camp News" service into wider areas beyond its early base in the Adirondacks was made possible by three important factors.

The most important of these was the cooperation of many people in the new areas who contributed news, pictures, information and advertising for the wider coverage.

The cooperation of the editor's family and friends in addressing and mailing the magazine and in free secretarial service was very important in keeping costs to a minimum. Mrs. Reed, Winifred, Elwyn, Ralph and Frederick took part in the addressing and mailing as each issue was ready for distribution. Many friends also cooperated on occasion.

Salary from churches which the editor served along with his work in the camps was used for necessary travel in the wider areas as the service of the "Lumber Camp News" was extended. These parishes included churches at Big Moose, Forestport, Inlet, Old Forge, Raquette Lake, Star Lake, Wanakena and other places in Northern New York.

110

"THE NORTHERN LOGGER"

"What do you plan to do ultimately with the 'Lumber Camp News'?" This question was addressed to the editor one day in April, 1951, by Douglas Philbrook of Gorham, New Hampshire, who was doing mechanical research for some paper companies, with headquarters at Gorham. Doug went on to say that the mechanization of logging jobs through the introduction of the chain saw, bulldozer, and other woods equipment had created the need for a magazine with technical information and that the "Lumber Camp News" was the only organization in the Northeast which had a foundation for such a developement.

Doug's statement was destined to become the center of serious thought and discussion for some months and to ultimately take its place alongside of a significant statement made by lumberjack Ross Harvey thirteen years earlier, "We ought to have our own newspaper in the camp."

The editor discussed the question with loggers, foresters and forest industry leaders in Northern New England, New York and Pennsylvania during the next few weeks and found favorable interest in such a project. Plans were made for a dinner meeting of such leaders at Tupper Lake, New York, on August 10, 1951, at the time of the Woodsmen's Field Day.

The variety of membership in this group was significant for future developments. Ten of the men represented forest industries. Three were from forestry colleges, two from the U. S. Forest Service, four from the New York State Conservation Department and four from the "Lumber Camp News."

The group thoroughly considered the need for such a publication, the changes which it would involve and the financial backing which would be needed. Most of those present thought it would be a desirable project but were skeptical of securing the financial backing which would be necessary. Plans were made for future meetings in Albany, New York, which was nearer the center of northeastern transportation. Such meetings were held in Albany in October, 1951, and January, 1952. Plans had progressed sufficiently by January, 1952, to set up an expanded circulation department with Miss Phebe King of Scipioville, New York, in charge. Plans were also started to redesign the publication under the leadership of Thomas O'Donnell of Boonville, New York.

Northeastern Loggers' Association Formed

Plans were made for a meeting in Albany on May 23, 1952. The men present voted unanimously to establish the Northeastern Loggers' Association and to become organizing directors of the new association. The group present included: John R. Curry of the U. S. Forest Service; Prof. James E. Davis of the College of Forestry at Syracuse, N. Y.; Howard A. Hanlon of Cotton-Hanlon; H. V. Hart of the St. Regis Paper Co.; Wayne C. Lewison of Draper Corp.; G. A. McGinnis of Employers Mutual; Gerald A. Pesez, of the International Paper Co.; Francis E. Smalley of the Eagle Square Corp. of Stockbridge, Vt., and Frank A. Reed, who was editor and publisher of "The Lumber Camp News."

These nine men, who met at Albany on May 23, voted to include also as organizing directors: James S. Elliott of Coudersport, Pa; C. S. Herr of the Brown Co.; William A. Lynn of West Virginia Pulp and Paper; Perry H. Merrill, who was State Forester in Vermont; Robert S. Monahan of Dartmouth College; A. D. Nutting, who was Forest Commissioner of Maine; Fred C. Simmons of the U. S. Forest Service; John W. Stock of the Emporium Forestry Company and Donald Swan of the Great Northern Paper Company.

Eight of the organizing directors came from New York State, three from New Hampshire, three from Pennsylvania, two from Maine and two from Vermont. Forest industries, the forestry colleges, the state forestry departments and the U. S. Forest Service were well represented in the membership.

The major project of the Logger's Association, at first, was the publication of a magazine which was changed from "Lumber Camp News" to "Northeastern Logger." Douglas Philbrook suggested the name. John Curry was elected President of the Association with Wayne C. Lewison as Vice-President. Frank Reed was chosen as Editor of "The Northeastern Logger" as he had been of "The Lumber Camp News."

The editor and directors went about the task of organizing "The Northeastern Logger" to more adequately serve the loggers, the forestry program and forest industries of the Northeast.

Selection of "Logger" Staff

The first step was the choice of a staff of associate editors who would help to organize the technical departments and make them effective instruments of information.

Prof. James E. Davis of the State University College of Forestry at Syracuse, New York, became the Forest Management Editor. He was later succeeded by Elmer Kelso of Hollingsworth and Whitney at Waterville, Maine. Mr. Kelso is now with the U. S. Forest Service at Laconia, New Hampshire, but has continued to edit his department.

Kenneth Barraclough, who was extension forester in New Hampshire,

112

became the Small Woodlot Editor. His wide experience in the field made him extremely well qualified.

Fred C. Simmons of the U. S. Forest Service at Upper Darby, Pa., became Logging Engineering Editor. His department included new machinery, as well as articles in his field. Leland Hooker of Michigan Tech at Houghton, Mich., later succeeded Mr. Simmons during his two year itinerary in South America.

Kenneth Compton of the State College of Forestry at Syracuse became Sawmill Editor for a while, but Prof. Orvel Schmidt of Penn State University succeeded him in that position. John Stock became Logging Safety Editor and was later succeeded by William Rutherford of Paul Smith's College. Rev. Thomas Carlisle became Sports Editor and Prof. A. B. Recknagel of Ithaca the Editor of Recent Publications. Mr. Recknagel was later succeeded by Prof. Robert Ashman of Augusta, Maine.

These associate editors wrote articles, secured articles from others and reviewed articles which were to be published in "The Northeastern Logger." This service was a significant factor in the growth of "The Logger."

An equally important problem was the establishment of an office with sufficient staff to carry on the work of the new project. This organization of an adequate staff was a bit difficult, as funds were very limited. The initial investment in addition to Frank Reed's gift of "The Lumber Camp News" was $1,105.00.

Under these conditions, the office was established for a time in The Woodsmen's Club at Old Forge where rent was free. June Ball of Old Forge served as office secretary on a half time basis for a while and later became full time secretary. Phebe M. King handled the circulation department in her home at Scipioville, New York, also on a part time basis. These two dedicated people, with the editor, made up the paid staff of "The Northeastern Logger" except that the editor drew no salary for the first two years. Mrs. Emily Weaver later succeeded June Ball as office secretary and has continued effectively in this position until the present time.

The addition of the associate editors and office staff made it possible for the editor to spend half of his time in the field calling on paper companies, sawmills, logging operators, forestry projects, forestry colleges, state forestry departments and National Forests. The other half of his time was spent on production of the magazine, necessary correspondence and attendance at important meetings.

The need of a more attractive magazine was soon evident. Leo Stahl, who had been an artist in New York City and had a summer hotel in the eastern Adirondacks, became the Art Director and greatly improved the appearance of the Logger. John Mahaffy of Boonville, New York, later

113

succeeded him as Art Director and has continued "The Logger" as an attractive magazine.

Mechanization of Woods Operations

The change from "Lumber Camp News" to "Northeastern Logger" turned out to be a strategic move in 1952. It came at a time when mechanization in the woods was underway and needed more direction which a publication could give. "The Northeastern Logger" soon became an important part of the mechanical revolution .

The mechanical revolution had other profound changes. It made possible the construction of roads to the log jobs and lumber camps which had not been possible in previous years. This road construction program eliminated the necessity of lumber camps and ultimately eliminated the camps.

The mechanization program also brought about a revolution in woods personnel. The old-time lumberjack, who had worked with such skill and dedication with tools of his time including the axe, the saw, the spud, the peavy and the horse, was replaced by younger men who were machine operators and were attracted to the woods by the new methods and equipment after World War II.

The mechanical changes in the woods and the resulting reduction of lumber camps also brought about a situation in 1954 when the editor-sky pilot was forced to make a decision. Should he return to a normal pastorate program such as he had at Old Forge some years earlier or should he continue in his association with logging, forestry and the forest industries in a different capacity as editor of "The Northeastern Logger." The decision was affected somewhat by the fact that there were not sufficient funds to employ a qualified editor. The decision was made to devote the next few years to editing "The Northeastern Logger," which included the Sky Pilot's Page. The lumberjack sky pilot became an editor and sky pilot over a wider area in mills, logging operations, forestry projects and forestry colleges instead of lumber camps.

The editor's travels led him through Northern New England where he became well acquainted with many who were operating sawmills, log jobs, pulpwood departments and the forest industries as well as a great many foresters in both industrial and private forestry. He was inspired to publish descriptions of operations in those areas and to gather material on operations in former years. Historical articles on the Penobscot River, the Connecticut Valley, the Kennebec, the Androscoggin, the Chemung, Lincoln, New Hampshire, and other areas made interesting reading along with information on logging, sawmilling and other major forestry problems.

114

The mechanical changes in logging and milling led to the establishment of an Annual Loggers' Congress in 1955. This is held in the spring season during a period when weather conditions in the woods bring the logging program to a halt. Its major features have included the technical sessions on logging and milling methods, an annual loggers' banquet, the annual meeting of the Loggers' Association and the demonstration of logging and milling equipment.

The Loggers' Congress has attracted several hundred men at each of its annual sessions and has contributed much in useful information.

The widening circle of travel on "The Logger" program brought the editor in touch with many interesting people and several new developments in the forest industries.

Pulp Chips from Slabs

One of these calls was made on Joe Wilner at Norway, Maine. Joe was installing a debarker in his wedgie heel plant there and was starting a chip manufacturing program to provide chips for the Brown Company at Berlin, New Hampshire. Joe developed this program with the co-operation of Mark Hamlin of the Brown Company and has been providing a growing supply since that time. Joe became very well known throughout the Northeast and was in great demand as a speaker on many occasions.

A call on John Eaton, who had a sawmill at Rochester, Vermont, indicated that John also was working on a program to produce chips from slabs and edgings on a large scale for use by the paper companies.

John's method was to establish a central chipping plant in a desirable location where it could chip the slabs and edgings from several neighboring sawmills. He designed a debarker for use in the individual sawmills so the logs could be debarked before they were sawed. The slabs and edgings were bound into large bundles after they left the saw and were shipped by truck to the central chipping plant. The bundles of slabs, which were held together with steel bands or heavy wire, were handled by fork lifts both at the sawmill and the chipping plant. Mr. Eaton established several of these chipping plants.

Lloyd Hawkensen of Ashland, New Hampshire, also developed central chipping plants to handle the slabs from adjacent mills. Some of the larger sawmills in the Northeast have built their own chippers at the mills.

Several additional men from Northern New England became active on The Logger's Association Board of Directors. These included; Harry Beach of the Oxford Paper Company at Rumford, Maine; Phil Chad-

115

bourne from the Chadbourne Lumber Company at Bethel, Maine; John Eaton of Rochester, Vermont; Frank Kennett of Conway, New Hampshire; Rand Stowell of Dixfield, Maine; Robert True of the S. D. Warren Company at Westbrook, Maine, and Henry Waldo of the Franconia Paper Company of Lincoln, New Hampshire. Both Harry Beach and Henry Waldo served effectively as President of The Logger's Association.

Increased efforts were made in Pennsylvania where the editor called on many mill operators including Marshall Case and Roy Cummings of Troy; George Patterson of Wellsboro; Russell Strange of Mansfield; Ben Kramer of Galeton; James Elliott, Thomas Leete of Coudersport; Tom Kennedy of Port Alleghany; William Faull of Bradford; Wendell McMillan of Sheffield; Russ Gustafson of Endeavor; E. A. Ponzer of St. Mary's; Mitstifer Brothers of Liberty; Oscar Dalton of Dubois; The Novosel Lumber Company of Kane; and William Young of Titusville. William Faull served as Association President for two years.

Journeys in Maryland and West Virginia

The editor's journeys led him also into Maryland where he made calls from the lumber companies on the eastern shore to the West Virginia Pulp and Paper Company at Luke and John Adams of the Western Maryland Railroad at Oakland. This area covered a wide variety of terrain and tree species within the woods of one state. John Adams became an active Loggers' Association Director over a period of several years.

Assistant State Foresters Al Allison and Lester McClung of West Virginia cooperated actively on plans for a visit in that state. Director Ephraim Olliver of the Monongahela National Forest and Sid Weitzman of the U. S. Forest Research Center at Elkins were all helpful in planning this trip. This was the first of several trips made to visit mills, logging operators and forestry projects in West Virginia.

One of his early calls was made on D. D. Brown at Elkins who had been an early lumberman in the area. He had come to West Virginia as a young man from Towanda, Pennsylvania.

The editor found that Howard Gray of the Meadow River Lumber Company at East Rainelle headed up the largest hardwood operation. Mr. Gray spent his life with the company and was thoroughly familiar with details of operation as well as company policy. He had moved up from saw filer to president of the company.

James P. Hamer of Kenova is another large lumber operator who has played a prominent role in the forest industry of the state and has been a leader in national organizations. Elmer Grimm of Terra Alta, George Myles of Elkins and consulting forester Jack Tillenghast of Madison

116

John E. Johnston pulpwood drive on the Jessup River.

Logging operator John E. Johnston and
camp clerk Joe Sirois.

Lumberjacks at lunch in cook camp.

Camp cook John McDonough preparing a meal.

Part of logging crew at camp at lunchtime.

Felling spruce with crosscut—
1942. *(Photo by Fynmore)*

Crosscut sawyers David Geer and Gilbert Engel furnish
excitement for spectators.

(Left to right) Frank Reed, Prof. William Rutherford, David Short, Rev.
James Getaz, Jr., V. Rev. Msgr. Robert A. Farmer, and Hubert Lee dedicate
monument in cemetery at Old Forge.

A Brown Company camp in the mid-forties.

Bill Burger *(left)* at camp on the Kennebego drive.

The Kennebego driving crew
breaking piles at the landing.

Boat crew fastening log boom
on Brown Company drive.

Bill Burger presents Bible to
New England lumberjack.

Sky pilot conducts an open air service on Kennebego drive.

have been active leaders among the recent mill operators in West Virginia. The list of mills included the Mower Lumber Company at Cass and the Cherry River Boom and Lumber Company of Richwood. The latter has now become part of the farflung Georgia-Pacific program.

Forest industry leaders in West Virginia have been making real progress in improving their mills and the program of wood utilization. They have introduced several new mills to better utilize the forest resources of the state. These new projects include the Burke-Parsons-Bowlby mill at Spencer which specializes in the treatment of poles and timbers, along with a sawmill, and the charcoal plant which Kingsford established at Parsons a few years ago. The new U. S. Forest Service Marketing Laboratory at Princeton will further advance the program of utilization and marketing of wood. The West Virginia University Forestry School at Morgantown is also making an important contribution to the forestry management and utilization program.

Development in the Lake States

"How much would it cost to send two hundred Christmas gift subscriptions of "The Northeastern Logger?" The voice at the other end of the telephone was that of Emmett Hurst, woodlands manager of Consolidated Papers at Wisconsin Rapids, Wisconsin. The price quotation was favorable and Mr. Hurst sent the order.

He added in the letter, "The tree species and problems in the Northeast and the Lake States are much the same. The Logger could serve both areas." Mr. Hurst suggested a change of name for the publication from Northeastern Logger to Northern Logger as more appropriate for the enlarged territory. The change to Northern Logger was made at the annual meeting of the Loggers' Association at Woodstock, Vermont, in April 1963.

Mr. Hurst's request and suggestion opened up the possibility of developing Logger service in the Lake States and the Central West. If there was to be circulation in that area, news coverage and articles would be needed to interest the readers. The editor decided on a trip and spent three weeks on a journey in Wisconsin and the Upper Peninsula. The paper industry was very important in the Wisconsin River Valley. The watershed control system in the area, which had been under the leadership of Merv Kyler, was fantastic. A number of paper companies, sawmills and other forest industries cooperated actively in providing useful information and illustrated articles.

Plans were made for a special Wisconsin issue of the Logger. Merv

117

Kyler of Wausau, who headed up the Wisconsin River Development program, ordered five thousand copies of this issue.

The visits in the Upper and Lower Peninsulas led to the publication of a Michigan issue which was distributed widely in that state. Michigan State University, Michigan Tech and the University of Michigan cooperated actively in furnishing articles and information, as did many industries in the state.

The editor believed that the intervening states should also be served by The Logger. He found keen interest in such a program on visits to Ohio, Indiana, Illinois and Kentucky. Later journeys in these four states led to special issuses for each of them with a high degree of cooperation in their preparation from state forestry departments, colleges, the U.S. Forest Services, loggers, foresters and forest industries.

The Indiana Hardwood Association, the Ohio Forestry Association the Appalachian Hardwood Association, The American Walnut Association and many others cooperated actively in providing interesting articles which were read by many subscribers over a wide area. The editor also concentrated efforts on some communities such as Jasper, Indiana, and Akron, Ohio, where unusual industrial developments had taken place. He also prepared a series of illustrated articles on major equipment manufacturers, many of whom are around the Great Lakes area.

Illness in New Hampshire

One morning, in 1959, the editor awakened early at his room in the Mount Madison Motel in Gorham, New Hampshire and discovered that he couldn't lift a shoe with his right hand. Investigation indicated that the same condition existed on the right side of his face. Apparently part of his right side was paralyzed. It was apparent also that there would be some delay in his morning call on C. S. Herr at the Brown Company in neighboring Berlin.

After a third effort, he succeeded in reaching the telephone at the motel office to inform Pat Herr of the reason for the delay. Pat sent Omer Lang and Joe Robischaud to pick up the editor. The Brown Company physician decided that a visit to the hospital would be necessary and diagnosed the illness as cerebral spasm.

A two day stay in the hospital at Berlin, New Hampshire, restored strength to the right hand and feeling to the editor's face. Joe Robischaud drove him back to his home in Old Forge, New York, where he was able to return gradually to his duties.

An emergency meeting of Loggers' Association officers was called to consider alternate plans for the publication of The Logger in case of a recurrence of the partial paralysis. The editor suggested that arrangements be made with William Charbonneau of Boonville, New York, to back him up in case of emergency. William served in that capacity for several years and was always familiar with the progress of The Loggers' publication in case the editor was permanently disabled.

Barnum and St. Paul, Minnesota

A five week trip to the Central West and the Lake States in the early summer of 1963 included visits in Minneapolis and St. Paul, Minnesota, where plans were made for a Minnesota issue of The Northern Logger. The School of Forestry, the State Forestry Department, the U.S. Forest Service, and several individuals cooperated enthusiastically to produce a highly interesting and informing Minnesota issue.

Highlights of the Minnesota trip were a weekend at Barnum, which is the same community where Frank Higgins began his ministry in the lumber camps sixty-eight years before, and a call in Duluth on Mrs. Herman Gurlock who came to Barnum on the same Sunday in 1895 that Frank Higgins began his ministry.

This Barnum visit completed the sixty-eight year cycle which had involved several sky pilots and thousands of old time lumberjacks who lived more meaningfully because Frank Higgins pioneered a great movement and gave real meaning to the term "Sky Pilot."

As the editor drew near to the close of his active program as editor of "The Northern Logger," he checked more carefully on activities of the period since he came to the North Woods, forty-eight years ago. These activities include:

Automobile travel in 29 cars—1,450,000 miles

Travel on foot in the woods—75,000 miles

Plane travel—Mileage unknown, in several types of planes ranging from the Piper Cub to the modern jet.

As the editor looks back over these years of service and association, he is very grateful for a variety of blessings including many beautiful views, inspiring associations, the challenge of opportunity, the enthusiastic cooperation of hundreds of people, the blessing of work and the Heavenly Father's protection and care in the midst of these journeys.

Fred C. Simmons was chosen to succeed the editor following his resignation. He concluded his services as editor on July 31, 1964, but still does some work on the Association program.

VI

WILLIAM J. BURGER, JR.

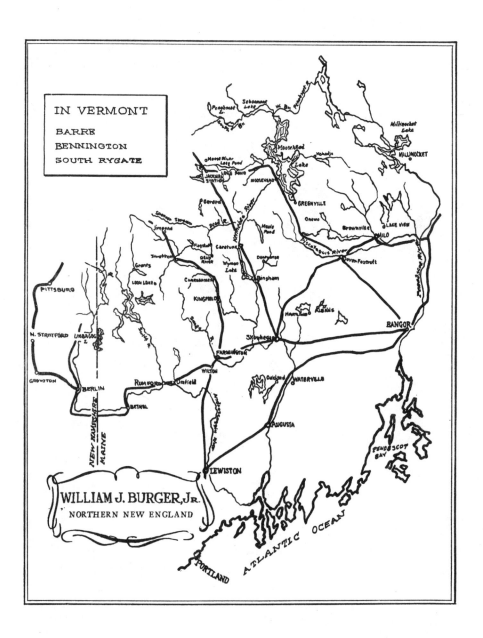

IN VERMONT

BARRE
BENNINGTON
SOUTH RYGATE

WILLIAM J. BURGER, JR.
NORTHERN NEW ENGLAND

WILLIAM J. BURGER, JR.

Early Life

Rev. William J. Burger, Jr., made his first visit to a lumber camp at Limekiln Lake near Inlet in the Adirondack Mountains in the late autumn of 1943. His later journeys took him to hundreds of lumber camps in Vermont, New Hampshire and Maine.

William was born and reared in Trenton, New Jersey, where he attended school and helped his father in the butcher shop.

He received his religious training in a Christian home and in the Westminster Presbyterian Church of Trenton. As a young men, he felt the call to greater service in the Christian ministry and continued his education at the College of Wooster in Wooster, Ohio, where many young men have received training for the ministry. He worked his way through college by washing dishes and helping in a butcher shop. His marriage to Miss Alice Starkweather of Columbus, Ohio, took place at the Starkweather home on June 16, 1935, which was the day before graduation.

Upon graduation from the College of Wooster in 1935, William became a student at Yale Divinity School in New Haven, Connecticut. Yale had several outstanding teachers and scholars on the faculty who helped to broaden the knowledge and stimulate the aspirations of the young student for the ministry. He found these to be fruitful years in both learning and Christian fellowship. A son, Douglas, was born in New Haven.

Mr. Burger accepted the call in 1938 to the First Presbyterian Church of Graniteville, Vermont, which is in the heart of the Barre granite area. Many of his parishioners were associated with the granite industry, and he was able to learn much from them about the problems of both the industry and the workmen.

The young minister's next move led him from the Vermont hills to the vicinity of New England's great metropolis. He was called in 1940 to the First Presbyterian Church of Haverhill, Massachusetts, which is a few miles from Boston. The new pastor went about his parish program in this suburban community with devotion and energy. He was especially active in the program of weekday religious education in the community. Two sons, William III and Richard were born at Haverhill.

During his years of devoted service in the parish at Haverhill, Mr.

Burger was unaware that the Lord was laying foundations for a new call that would later challenge his best skill and energy.

In 1942, Frank Reed asked New York Synod's committee on National Missions to make a second five-year study of the Adirondack Lumber Camp Parish program to check on its progress and its needs for expansion. This study indicated that the possibilities of extending the parish into the lumber camps of Northern New England was a real challenge which would involve the addition of at least one more sky pilot and the close cooperation of the Synods of New York and New England.

Sky Pilot in the Lumber Camps

Synod executives Walter Knight of New England and Howard Yergin of New York made plans for the cooperation of the two Synods in the project. Mr. Knight suggested Rev. William Burger, Jr., of Haverhill, Massachusetts, as the man best qualified for the new position. His knowledge of Northern New England indicated that he would be a desirable man to expand the lumber camp parish in that area.

William made a short visit to the Adirondacks with headquarters briefly at the Woodsmen's Club in Forestport. He made a visit with Frank Reed to the C. J. Strife lumber camp at Limekiln Lake where he participated in the service and gave his first sermon in a lumber camp bunkhouse.

William's reaction to the new challenge as sky pilot to lumberjacks was favorable. After a meeting with Synodical executives Howard Yergin and Walter Knight, he was chosen as the new sky pilot and began his ministry in the Adirondacks on February 1, 1944, with headquarters at the Woodsmen's Club.

His first visit was made to the John E. Johnston camps on the Jessup River where he conducted two lumber camp services on his own while his senior partner was visiting some other camps farther back on the Jessup River.

The new sky pilot continued to visit lumber camps in the Adirondacks and the Tug Hill area through the hauling season of 1944. He became acquainted with many men in the Finch Pruyn camps at Newcomb, the Gould Paper Company camps on Tug Hill and several other places. He was well received by the men who greatly appreciated his services. The fact that the men in the camps called him "Bill" Burger was indicative of his reception in the camps. The usage of the name has continued in the New England camps and in his other associations.

"You're damn right," said an Austrian lumberjack in one of the Adirondack lumber camps as Bill delivered his sermon in the bunkhouse

124

one evening. The sudden comment was a bit startling to the new sky pilot who had to return to the beginning of his sermon to pick up the thread of thought. However, the lumberjack's comment was in dead earnest, a fact which Bill came to appreciate as he continued his ministry in the camps. It was the lumberjack's way of saying, "Amen."

Move to Vermont

Bill helped with the program at the Woodsmen's Club as the log haul came to a close, including the Woodsmen's Club Second Annual Dinner. After that, he returned to New England and made plans to move his family to South Ryegate, Vermont, where he made headquarters for the next four years beginning in May 1944. The name of the parish was changed from the Adirondack to the Northeastern Lumber Camp parish.

His Adirondack visits were made to lumber camps in known locations where the route of approach could be described by his senior partner. His Northern New England trips, at first, were journeys of discovery to find out where the camps were located and the best way of approach. His early trips in Vermont included visits to the John E. Johnston camp near Bennington, Vermont, on a Finch Pruyn and Company operation where Floyd Miklic was a foreman. He and Floyd became good friends.

Bill soon added two new features to the program in the lumber camps as he had observed it in the Adirondacks. He purchased a sound moving picture machine and an electric generator to furnish power for it when electric power was not available in a camp. He also secured complete Bibles in various languages which men in the camps might purchase at a modest price.

He took an active part in developing the service of the "Lumber Camp News" in the lumber camps of Vermont and New Hampshire.

Sometimes Bill had to learn his travel information the hard way. The first time he visited the Waterville Valley in the White Mountain National Forest, he asked walking boss Leonard Thibadault the way to Cascade Camp. Leonard told him to drive to the winter camp, leave his car there and hike the toteroad the remaining three miles to camp. Leonard neglected to tell him that the toteroad led up the steep side of a rocky mountain and that it was exposed to the hot August sun all the way. Bill found the travelling difficult and never forgot the experience.

He soon observed that the major part of the operating lumber camps in Vermont and New Hampshire were company or contractor's camps built to supply pulpwood for the major paper companies of the area, including the Brown Company of Berlin, the Groveton Paper Company of Groveton, the International Paper Company, the Parker-Young Company of Lincoln and the St. Regis Paper Company which had extensive operations around Pittsburg.

On a trip to the Phillips Brook operations of the International Paper Company, the French-Canadian camp blacksmith made the new sky pilot feel welcome by saying, "Hello minister, I am glad to see you. I looked down the road and said, 'That is the little minister coming'."

Parker-Young Camp Visits

A trip to the Parker-Young operations at Lincoln, New Hampshire, brought him into contact with Woodlands Manager Henry Waldo who had succeeded Sherman Adams. He also visited the camp where Frank McCormack was the foreman and had a long visit with Frank at the camp office. Frank later said to him, "Come back soon. In the two years I have been in camp, you are the first man who has come along just to visit." This led to a lasting friendship between Bill and Frank. When Frank left Lincoln to become walking boss for the Atlas Plywood Company in the Howland, Maine, area, he invited his new friend to make him a visit, an invitation which led the sky pilot to visit lumber camps in that area of Maine.

One day when Bill was visiting at Frank McCormack's Camp 8 on the Lincoln Line, a lumberjack dropped dead as he walked from the cook camp to the lobby. Frank said to Bill, "This isn't my department. You will have to take over." Bill called the woodland office and made arrangements for the transfer of the woodsman to the undertaking parlor.

One day Bill went into a camp of the Parker-Young Company and laid out a display of Bibles on the bunkhouse table. One man said, "I'll bet you don't have any Bibles in my language—Slovenian." Bill didn't but promised to get one for the man and another for his friend from the American Bible Society.

When the Slovenian Bibles arrived, Bill took the two of them to camp early one evening and found his friend who ordered them deep in a poker game, with a pile of money in front of him. The man asked how much they were and paid Bill for the Bibles from his pile of poker earnings as he and his companions continued the game.

The Parker-Young Company was later sold to a new owner and is now the Franconia Paper Company. Henry Waldo is still the Woodlands Manager.

Brown Company Camps

The Brown Company of Berlin, New Hampshire, had extensive pulpwood operations in several areas. They had an operations headquarters at

126

the Brown Farm where Joe Mooney kept the telephone exchange and supervised the distribution of camp supplies. They also had a storehouse at Cupsuptic where camps around the neighboring lakes were supplied by boats. There was an operation also at Mill Stream near Shellburne and another near Erroll.

The young sky pilot found a friendly spirit at the Brown Company office on the part of C. S. Herr, Myles Standish, Omar Lang and others, as well as the operations superintendents, foremen, clerks, cooks and men in the camps. This offered the opportunity for an active program in the camps and extensive travels over the area.

On one of these trips Bill had an exciting experience. He started out on a camp trip from Cupsuptic storehouse in the company supply boat known as "The Stub." After Captain Bernard Otis had started the eighteen-mile journey across the lake, Bill discovered that the cargo consisted of four boxes of dynamite, two drums of gasoline and one scared clergyman.

Another day which the sky pilot remembers well is a camp visit on D-Day in June, 1945, when he and some members of the crew heard over the radio the news and the call of the President to gather in their churches for prayer. He announced that the prayer service would be held in the recreation room at that large camp. Every man possible crowded into that room and others who could not get in stood outside while the sky pilot conducted a short service of prayer and worship which was a very meaningful experience for both pastor and worshippers.

Bill had many interesting experiences in the Brown Company camps. On one trip to the Brown Farm he met Brown Company's chief cook, Fred Armstrong, who rode with him on his journey upstream to the drive. As they continued on the journey Fred said, "I'll need to stop and see Eddie at Kennebago Wangin. I have a letter for him from the girls at the doctor's office."

When they arrived at the Wangin, Fred produced the letter, which was covered with lipstick kisses from the girls at the office, and gave it to Eddie. The letter brought the anticipated cheer. Six months later Eddie married the girl who had sent the letter. They have had a happy and successful married life.

Bill had one of his most inspiring experiences at the close of a service in the open air at Mill Brook Camp in Shellburne, New Hampshire, where one hundred and twenty-five men viewed his movies, listened to his sermon and bowed their heads reverently in prayer. As he viewed the cross and the flag against the background of the surrounding woods and the setting sun, he felt vividly the sense of the Heavenly Father's presence and thanked Him for the opportunity of a ministry in such beautiful country and among such sincere and dedicated men.

Shortly after that, Bill made a statement reflecting the basic concepts of his ministry in the camps. He said. "The themes of which I preach are those which all men need; prayer, surrender to God, temptation, faithfulness to the best we know. Never have I said anything in a service or private conversation which would encourage a man to be loyal to any church save that of this birth or prior choice. I consider it a great boon to worship together with men of all creeds in America."

One camp foreman came back from town slightly intoxicated, which is somewhat unusual in the camps, and didn't want Bill to conduct a service in the bunkhouse. Finally, he said. "I'll have the men vote on it." The cook took the vote of the crew and reported that all but two in the large crew wanted the service.

When they made a cut on the Dead River, Bill was inquiring about the location of camps. They advised him not to go back to one camp which was quite a distance, in part, because the crew would not be interested. Bill arrived before lunch and arranged a display of Bibles, largely in French, on the bunkhouse table. When he returned from lunch to the bunkhouse, every Bible from the display was being read eagerly.

One morning while traveling on a winter hauling road, Bill stopped to talk with two road monkeys who were building their fire to heat the sand for the sand hill. One of them soon spoke of his friends coming out for breakfast and stepped out into the deep snow with his axe to fell a cedar tree. After a careful look to see if there was any danger, the deer also waded out to have a good breakfast on the cedar tree which the road monkey had cut for their pleasure.

Forest Fires in 1947

The autumn of 1947 brought a very dry season which created hazardous conditions in all of the forests in the Northeast and particularly in Northern New England.

One day the sky pilot went to visit the Flume Brook Camp on the Parker-Young operations. He found the office locked and no sign of life around except in the cook camp where the cook was busy preparing a meal for the crew which was out on a fire-fighting operation. He found the same conditions existing around Stark, Maine, where he went to run movies in a rural parish. Most of the meetings had to be postponed. The men were all out fighting fire as they were also on the serious fires at Bar Harbor, Brownville and other places in Maine and other parts of New England.

The sky pilot had only arrived back home when he and his wife thanked God for a great blessing. The rain had begun to fall and rain alone could bring satisfactory control of great forest fires which had caused so much damage that year.

The serious forest fire condition of 1947 did have one good result. It caused the states of the Northeast to consider better ways of forest fire control and brought them together in a combined effort called "The Compact" under the leadership of Arthur Hopkins. In this combined effort, the Northeastern states standardized their fire-fighting equipment and methods so that neighboring states could rush suddenly to the assistance of one which had an acute forest fire emergency such as Maine had had in the autumn of 1947. State Forester Austin Wilkins and Fred Holt of Maine were active leaders in a new type of training program which better prepared men for the handling of major forest fires.

Developments in Maine

The years 1947 and 1948 brought some important changes in the sky pilot's program in Northern New England. He had became thoroughly familiar with the lumber camps in Vermont and New Hampshire and had made many visits to those camps. Now he began to push his camp visitation program farther eastward into Maine where there were many camps in operation and several thousand men at work in the camps.

Part of this movement came through the invitations of Frank McCormack and other friends who moved to operations in Maine. Some of it came because other Maine operations such as those of the Great Northern Paper Company centering at Pittston Farm were not far from Brown Company operations in the Rangely Lake area. Bill found a friendly spirit among the company executives, foremen and men in the camps. He extended his visits to the Moosehead Lake area and the Upper Penobscot as well as around Pittston.

Hollingsworth & Whitney also had extensive pulpwood operations and many lumber camps in the Upper Kennebec and Dead River areas. The sky pilot found his way into these camps as he did also in many of the International Paper Company camps in Northern Maine. Many of the International camps provided pulpwood for the mills at Ticonderoga and Corinth in northeastern New York. Wherever, he went, he found a warm welcome. Men enjoyed his interesting movies, his news comments and his short sermons. They joined with the sky pilot in reverent prayers in the bunkhouses throughout the North Woods.

Move to New Boston

Bill and his family decided that it was wise also to move his headquarters farther eastward to be near the center of operations. A question by the children, "Will daddy be home this weekend?" stimulated consideration of the move. In 1948 he moved from South Ryegate, Vermont, to New Boston, New Hampshire.

He arranged to supply a parish in New Boston as he had done at South Ryegate. This kept him in touch with the people and program of a normal parish and brought him back to his home on weekends from his long journeys in the lumber camp.

His increasing familiarity with Northern New England and its people brought an increasing number of invitations to speak at schools, churches, service clubs and other places. Some of these invitations led him to more distant states such as New Jersey, Ohio, North Carolina and Georgia, where many people wanted to know about life in the lumber camps of the north. However, Bill spent as much time as possible in the lumber camps over an increasingly wide area.

Bill went about his activities in his wide parish with dedication and energy from his headquarters at New Boston, New Hampshire, during the six-year period from 1948-1954. He observed certain important changes in the logging program during that period. One of these was that the World War II era and that immediately following brought greater mechanization to the woods. The chainsaw very largely replaced the crosscut and the bucksaw. The bulldozer opened up new roads for the use of trucks in transporting logs and pulpwood. The tractor gradually replaced the horse as a method of skidding logs. Young men who were machine operators came into the woods after World War II to replace the old-time lumberjack who had worked with so much skill and dedication with the tools of his generation such as the saw, the axe, the peavy, the spud, the horse, the waterbox and the heavy hauling sleighs.

Changes in the Woods

Lumber camps began to disappear in many parts of Northern New England as they did in New York and the Lake States. A mechanical revolution had brought many changes to the woods including changes in personnel and in the mode of living. Many of the younger men lived at home and drove back and forth to the jobs.

There are some areas, however, where lumber camps still prevail. These are areas which are farther removed from public highways and where the rivers can still be used to advantage for the driving of softwood pulpwood. Such an area is Northern Maine where many lumber camps still prevail. These have continued to make a broad parish for the sky pilot's efforts and journeys.

These changes in logging methods and woods personnel made 1954 a year of decision for Bill Burger as it was for the writer.

The concentration of the remaining lumber camps in Northern Maine and Northern New Hampshire meant that parish headquarters at New Boston, New Hampshire, was too far removed from the center of parish operations. A move farther north and east seemed desirable.

The presence of younger logging and pulpwood operators in their homes in rural communities of Northern New England meant that some attention should be given to those communities. As farms were deserted and land returned to woods, the communities were often left in a poor economic situation. The churches in these declining communities were having a serious struggle and many of them had given up the struggle for existence.

There were some signs of life and hope among the small rural parishes of Central Maine however. Several men had consecrated their lives to the rural ministry and were giving the parishes competent and dedicated leadership. This group of men included Carl Geories at Leeds and Charles Reid at Kingfield. Many of the lay people in the parishes also caught the vision of new life in the rural churches and were dedicating their talents and resources to its more fruitful ministry. They were approaching these objectives from an interdenominational viewpoint.

Move to Farmington, Maine

Bill Burger decided to cast in his lot with these parishes in Central Maine along with the work in the lumber camps. In 1955 he purchased a house in Farmington, Maine, which has served both as a home for his family and headquarters for his parish. The location was more desirable than New Boston, New Hampshire, as it was quite near to the lumber camps in Northern Maine.

Bill Burger, Carl Geories, Charles Reid and Dean Bembower led their parishes in the establishment of "The Mission at the Eastward," which includes thirteen rural parishes and the Northeastern Lumber Camp Parish. It includes three of the major denominations. They organized a Parish Council composed of two laymen from each parish along with the clergymen involved, to plan and carry out the parish program.

The Parish Council purchased a farm near the village of Stark. They used the farmhouse as a manse for the local minister and put the farm

131

to a variety of uses. The farm is now the site of a summer camp which acts as the home for three summer camp sessions. The nine buildings in the camp have been planned and constructed by skilled laymen from the parishes. Camp leadership is also furnished by clergymen and lay leaders from the parishes.

Open fields on the farm have been planted with red and white pine. The farm forest has been marked for selective cutting by a trained forester and will furnish lumber for additional buildings and facilities.

Bill Burger has furnished leadership for the Fairmont Church on the edge of Farmington. He divides his time among three major projects: the lumber camps in Northern Maine and Northern New Hampshire, the Fairmont Church where he carries on a regular program of worship services and Christian education, and leadership in the Mission at the Eastward. He finds this both a varied and exciting program.

During his twenty-two years of ministry in Northern New England, Bill Burger has travelled 650,000 miles by automobile and many miles on foot, has conducted 1,850 services in lumber camps, has called on hundreds of families and has given hundreds of addresses and sermons in churches, schools, service clubs and other places. He has also made several speaking tours in more distant places such as Pennsylvania, Ohio, North Carolina, Georgia and Missouri.

Bill Burger considers it a real privilege to have labored in the lumber camps and rural areas of Northern New England. The people of his broad parish are equally grateful for his ministry among them.

VII

THE SKY PILOT'S PAGE

The Sky Pilot's Page had its roots in the brief prayers and short devotional articles which the *Lumber Camp News* carried during the years of its operation from 1939 to 1952. When *The Lumber Camp News* became *The Northeastern Logger*, these articles and prayers were condensed into one page known as The Sky Pilot's Page. The following articles were taken from twelve issues of *The Northeastern* and *Northern Logger*.

GOALS FOR THE NEW YEAR

"Forgetting the things which are behind, and reaching forth unto the things which are before, I press toward the mark of the high calling of God in Christ Jesus."

The Apostle Paul, who wrote these words in his interesting letter to the church at Philippi in ancient Macedonia, was a man of remarkable achievements. One marvels at his ability to travel so far, endure so much and to reach such a high level of achievement.

The above words taken from the letter give a partial clue to his greatness.

Paul was a man who was not worried about the past. In times gone by, some of his deeds had been unworthy but he believed that God, through Christ, forgave his sins. He could say, on one occasion, "Christ Jesus came into the world to save sinners of whom I am chief."

This lack of worry about the past gave him energy for the present and insight for the future. He could face the future instead of the past. He was continually "reaching forward to those things which were before."

But the future had meaning to Paul because he had a goal which he expressed in these terms, "I press toward the mark of the high calling of God in Christ Jesus."

Following his remarkable experience on the Damascus Road, Paul could never be a drifter. As a follower of Christ he had to be a pursuer of the High Way. "The High Calling of God in Christ Jesus" became the goal of his striving. Toward that goal he pressed with increasing effort. For the achievement of that goal he gave his best in thought, activity and sacrifice.

The experience and words of Paul provide a background against which we may face the year with its struggles, hardships and challenges. We can look upon the old year without worry, for in Christ, we find the way to forgiveness.

In the spirit of Paul, we look forward to the tasks and experiences of the New Year with hope and anticipation. It may bring some hardships, discouragement

A PRAYER

O God, who controls the destinies of men, we thank Thee for the abundant blessings which the old year has brought; for fine associations, opportunities to learn new truth, the chance of constructive service, the land of liberty in which we live and daily evidence of Thy mercies.

Forgive us, we pray, for our lack of concern for the happiness of others, for our tendency to seek our own pleasures, for our failure to measure up to the high standard which we find in Christ.

We are grateful for opportunities and challenges of the New Year. Help us to face its trials and discouragements with great courage and sublime faith. Enable us also to see with clarity some great goals which we may pursue with keen anticipation, persistent effort and renewed consecration.

We ask this in Jesus' name.

Amen.

and suffering but God's Grace is sufficient for every need. His strength is made perfect in weakness. The year will also bring rich associations, great friendships, a large measure of Divine Love and opportunities for great achievement.

The New Year will come to us with deeper meaning if we, like Paul, have some great goals toward which we strive with courage and determination. Perhaps we, like him, will find those goals in "The high calling of God in Christ Jesus."

Those great goals give meaning to our daily task. It is a chance to earn a living for ourselves and families and much more. It is also the opportunity to serve God and our fellowmen.

Those goals will give purpose also to our leisure time and activities. These too will be spent for the service of God, the enrichment of human life and the welfare of the nation.

AMERICA, THE BEAUTIFUL

O beautiful for spacious skies
For amber waves of grain,
For purple mountain majesties
Above the fruited plain!
America! America!
God shed His grace on thee
And crown thy good with brotherhood
From sea to shining sea.

This familiar hymn from the pen of Katherine Lee Bates expresses profound appreciation for many commendable elements in American life, some of which are found in the realm of nature and natural resources.

Miss Bates was born in 1859 and died in 1929. During most of her life, she was a professor of English Literature at Wellesley College, near Boston, Mass.

Apparently the writing of this hymn grew out of a trip which Miss Bates took in 1893 to visit the Columbian Exposition in Chicago and the Rocky Mountain region in Colorado. One of the interesting journeys in Colorado was to the summit of Pike's Peak which is a little more than 14,000 feet in elevation.

Her view of the skies from Pike's Peak brought to a climax her appreciation of the solar system and the distant stars, many of which are suns with their own solar system. As she had done on other occasions, she

135

watched the setting sun shining on the floating clouds as they shone with brilliant yellow, then changed to orange, red and purple and faded away into gray.

On her journey from Chicago to Colorado, the author of this hymn traveled by train through the great wheat and corn fields of Iowa and Nebraska. She had seen the fields of waving wheat almost ripe reaching away as far the eye could see. She saw those fields of grain in terms of beauty and their value for food and thanked God for them.

From her perch at the top of Pike's Peak, Miss Bates looked out upon many interesting and beautiful things in the scene around her. The flat land reaching away to the eastward was once a sagebrush country but was now producing fruits and vegetables. Fertilizer and irrigation had made it a fruitful country. Around her, not far from Pike's Peak, were other rugged mountains. As she looked toward the west, she could see the western range of the Rockies with several majestic snow-covered peaks. This, no doubt, came as a climax to other mountain climbing trips in the East where the mountains had a greater variety of trees and of color. She expressed appreciation for the purple mountain majesties.

But Katherine Bates saw other great factors in American life. She lived only a short distance from Plymouth, where the Pilgrims had landed. No doubt her ancestors were among that group. She had a proper respect for these Pilgrims and the foundation they had laid for a life of freedom. On her westward journey, she saw that the descendants of those Pilgrims had beaten a path for freedom across the prairies and the wilderness.

She saw how many men and women had sacrificed to make human liberty a vital force in their own lives and the lives of others. She saw how some of them were people of prophetic spirit who dreamed of the dawn of a better day.

Katherine Lee Bates loved her country deeply and was very proud of it. She had a deep appreciation of its resources and beauty and the strength of its people. But she wanted her country to be a greater and a better nation. This hymn contains several brief prayers such as these: "God shed His grace on thee," "God mend thine every flaw," "May God thy gold refine." She loved her country so much that she prayed and taught and worked that it might be, in larger measure, the land of the free and the home of the brave.

THE CHANGE WHICH EASTER BROUGHT

The dawn of the first Easter Sunday found the early Christians in a state of despair and deep sorrow.

They had lost their best friend, a young man with whom they had been closely associated over a period of several years. Their sorrow was made deeper because this friend was a young man in the prime of life and his death had come through a violent and painful experience on the Cross, at the hands of bitter enemies.

But their despair went far deeper than sorrow. This young man had been the one around whom their life's program had revolved for many months. They looked upon Him as the one who understood both the nature of God and the destiny of man. They had found in His teaching and daily life the way to noble living and useful service. He made them aware of God's presence and taught them to dedicate their lives more completely to the service of God and their fellowmen. In Him, they found forgiveness and the power to live upon a higher plane. He supplied the great motives which became the driving force of their lives. He gave them hope for the dawn of a New Day under his leadership.

Now, that teacher was gone. His life had been snuffed out through this violent death on a cross. Their hopes for the future were blown to the four winds. Their motive for living had disintegrated. Life seemed totally hopeless. They were in a state of despair.

The hopelessness of the situation was reflected in the faces and conversation of two of them as they walked to Emmaus, which was about eight miles distance from Jerusalem. Even the stranger who joined them on the journey could see that there was some great cause for a sad expression in their faces. He inquired as to the cause and found them ready to relate the violent experience of their leader and friend.

But the earth-shaking events of that first Easter Sunday lifted them out of their despair. They became aware that

A PRAYER

O God, the source of every blessing, we are grateful for the coming of the spring season, with its promise of new life; for the melting snow, the green grass, the unfolding leaves, the open lakes and the spring flowers.

We thank Thee also for the coming of the Easter season and for its significance in the lives of men and in human history; for the open grave and the risen Christ, for its inspiring influence in the lives of the early Christians who were lifted out of their despair, for the fresh vitality which these men brought to the life of the ancient world and its enduring influence through the centuries.

Make us aware of the dynamic leadership of the Risen Christ, Grant that, also, under His leadership, we, also, may rise to higher levels of achievement, nobler ways of living, a fuller dedication of our lives to Thy service and greater confidence in life's eternal values.

We ask this in Jesus' name.

Amen.

137

Jesus had conquered death. He still lived, could walk with them on their journey and lead them through sorrow to joy. They said one to another at the end of the Emmaus journey, "Did not our hearts burn within us as He talked to us on the way and opened to us the Scriptures?"

The Resurrection meant that He was still a living leader who would lead them on to higher levels of achievements and the establishment of His kingdom. He still supplied the motive for living and the driving force which would make this message a transforming influence in the lives of men and in the course of human history.

Under His leadership, these early Christians went out, with enthusiasm, in every direction to preach the gospel. Peter went to the home of the Roman Centurion to baptize this leader and his family. Philip went into Samaria and brought great joy to that city. Thomas travelled eastward to India and established a Christian community, which has continued effectively through the centuries until the present time.

Easter Sunday also inspired their hopes for personal immortality. In an upper room in Jerusalem on the night before His death, the Great Teacher had said to His followers: "In my Father's house are many mansions. I go to prepare a place for you. I will come again and receive you unto myself." At the time, this probably came to their ears with only vague meaning.

The resurrection experience three days later brought home the full meaning of His words. They had realized the experience about which He had told them. Here was evidence that human personality was indestructible, that Christian personality was eternal, that death was swallowed up in victory.

"THE HEAVENS DECLARE THE GLORY OF GOD"

This article is being written above the clouds on a jet trip from New York to Dallas, Texas. The climb from Idlewild Airport to higher elevation was achieved quickly and with little apparent effort on the part of the jet.

We are now traveling at an elevation of 31,000 feet and are in constant sunshine, though the temperature outside may be below zero. The clouds underneath us were thick over West Virginia where a storm area prevailed. There are now only some floating clouds as we move over Western Kentucky.

From this elevation, one can see for many miles in every direction. The cumulus clouds in the distance on every side make a beautiful scene in the bright sunlight. In a few places, shafts of clouds rise above the general level of the clouds surrounding them.

Some features of the earth are evident also underneath us. The larger rivers are particularly visible. Highways and railroads are also evident. Farm buildings dot the countryside but seem pretty small from this elevation.

Green grass and grain fields lend richness to the scene, which is enhanced also by the evergreen and hardwood forests which cover the hillsides. Both of these are evidence of the great national resources which are a source of great beauty but also of the products of the soil and forest. These help to give America a high standard of living and contribute toward making it a great nation.

As I continue to write, we are approaching Memphis, Tennessee. Here our elevation seems to indicate that we are already beginning our descent to the Dallas airport, though we are still many miles away. The streets are becoming quite clear as we approach the city.

As one travels above the clouds, he recalls the words of the ancient Psalmist, "The heavens declare the glory of God and the firmament showeth His handiwork." The Psalmist undoubtedly gave expression to these feelings as he looked up and out at a beautiful sunset. He watched with keen interest and faith as the brilliant orange on the horizon turned to red, then purple and finally faded away into gray.

This beauty which the Psalmist saw from the earth as he looked upward is even more apparent as one looks down and out upon the clouds from our high elevation.

One marvels at man's achievements in the invention and production of many useful machines, including this jet plane which flies with such apparent ease far above the clouds on its quick trip to distant places. Man's research efforts and inventive genius have led him to use much more of the forces and resources of the world around him to enrich his own life and the lives of others.

These achievements have also made it possible for him to view with greater appreciation the spiritual force which has created the universe and sustains it from age to age. The passenger on the jet liner should be able to say with greater meaning. "The heavens declare the glory of God."

DEMOCRACY'S CHALLENGE IN OUR DAY

On July 4, 1776, Liberty Bell in Independence Hall rang out the news that the Declaration of Indendence had been signed by John Hancock. A new nation had been born. Perhaps it would be more correct to say that a young nation had broken the apron strings of the Mother Country. It had now arrived at the age of development where it had to face its own responsibilities.

In the years that followed that momentous event, the new nation struggled long and hard to carry its responsibilities including a war with the mother country, the organization of a new government, the development of foreign relations and the laying of suitable financial foundations.

We marvel at the courage of these men who pressed forward in the midst of so many obstacles. We marvel even more at the insight of men who could lay the foundations of a strong central government but, at the same time, guarantee the rights and freedom of the individual citizen.

This provision for human freedom was based upon a Christian concept of the worth of the individual, which is a basic concept in all Democracy. We believe the individual citizen has the ability to understand the issues of his time and to decide them with sound judgment. Freedom of speech, freedom of the press, freedom of worship and the right to vote are all important phases of that concept.

Built upon this foundation, America has grown as a Democracy. It has been a striking example of the growth of the democratic way of life and, at the same time, has encouraged other nations in the pursuit of democracy.

In recent times, Democracy has been under fire from several sources. One of these has been the growth of autocratic government in various parts of the world. Autocratic government is based upon the theory that only the rulers can

A PRAYER

O God, who controls the destiny of nations, we thank Thee for the land in which we live; for the extent and richness of its natural resources, for the pioneering spirit of those who settled on its shores, for the insight and courage of those men who laid its foundation in Liberty and Democracy, for the determination of those who braved dangers to settle its new territory, and for the courage of those men who gave their lives that America might live.

Enable us to match the insight, the courage and strength of these men of earlier times and to build well upon their foundations. Help us to use the nation's resources wisely, to see the issues of our time clearly, to value freedom and strengthen the foundations of democracy, to face the dangers of the future with calm courage and determination.

Grant that America may become a greater and a better nation where freedom survives and democracy prevails.

We ask this in Jesus' name.

Amen.

140

understand the issues of the time. The function of the individual citizen is to obey. The individual citizen lives for the good of the state, whereas, in democratic government, the state exists for the welfare and happiness of the individual.

Democracy is also, at times, under fire from within. Perhaps the most serious of the dangers within is lack of interest in vital issues on the part of the individual citizen. Autocratic government makes its greatest advances in those areas and periods where the individual citizen "let's George do it."

Race and class divisions also create the kind of climate in which the progress of democracy is difficult. Vital Democracy values the rights and independence of the individual regardless of race or class.

The development of a strong and virile democracy in our day involves several positive measures. These include:

1. Maintaining sufficient strength to stand courageously before the bully who would crush the individual in his pursuit of autocratic power.
2. Informing ourselves on the issues of our time and voting upon them with intelligent understanding and sound judgment.
3. Keeping at the focus of attention the real worth of the individual and insisting upon his rights for ourselves and others.
4. Participating actively in the affairs of the community and the state including the willingness to serve in public offices.

These steps will help us to build and to strengthen democratic processes in our own community and the nation.

STEWARDSHIP OF OUR FOREST RESOURCES

This article is being written along the Penobscot River north of Old Town, Maine, at a spot where the still water is flowing slowly by. A great expanse of woodland stretches to the westward as far as the eye can see.

In this quiet spot, one reminisces about the earlier scenes which took place on the Penobscot during the days when Old Town was the center of a great sawmill industry. Bangor was the nation's leading center for lumber shipments and the Penobscot was the scene of great log drives down to the mills as well as an important lumber rafting program from the mills to Bangor. These were the days when the God-given resources of the forest and the industry of men were cooperating to furnish lumber for the growth of a nation and for export to other areas.

The God-given resources of the forest and the industry of men have continued to be highly important in the Penobscot Valley and the State of Maine. The forest industries are, by far, Maine's largest and most important industry. 87% of the state's land area is supporting forests and more land may be returned from agriculture to forest in the years ahead.

As one looks upon this river scene and to the great forests beyond, he is inspired to offer thanks for the great beauty of the scene, for the resources of the forest and the insight and industry of men who have used these resources wisely for the happiness of people, the strength of the nation and the glory of God.

But this quiet scene may also be a place of dedication. It can inspire a prayer that we may have insight to use these resources more wisely for the scenic beauty of the countryside, an inspiring program of recreation and the development of forest products for the increased use of people and the continued strength of the nation. It may remind one that God is the real owner of the forest and we are his stewards who have to provide all of these benefits for people from His vast resources.

The writer is reminded of the statement of one forest land owner after he and the editor had taken an interesting journey through his 10,000 acre forest. This man remarked, "I am the fourth generation on this farm. I want to pass it on to my boys better than I found it."

This man had a fertile farm and an active sawmill in addition to his 10,000 acre woodlot. He made varied use of the forest including lumber and other wood products, a well rounded program of forest recreation and many places with great scenic beauty. His deep appreciation of the forest meant that he used it wisely as a good steward.

When this man died some time later, the writer found that he had been an active member of the school board, a dedicated officer of the church, and a leader in the Boy Scout movement. His appreciation of the forest had been part of a deep sense of spiritual values which had given meaning to all of his activities, including the sawmill and the forest.

THE GOSPEL OF LABOR

"This is the Gospel of Labor,
Ring it ye bells of the kirk;
The Lord of Love came down from above
To dwell with the men who work."

These words from the pen of the poet bring home the evident fact that Jesus was a person who worked and who understood the problems of working people in all walks of life.

Through several years He worked with His hands in the carpenter shop of Joseph in Nazareth. There He learned, no doubt, to construct buildings, such furniture as was used in the houses, vehicles and especially yokes for the oxen. His reference to yokes indicates that the building of them might have been a specialty in the carpenter shop. There, the growing boy learned that a well fitted yoke was the best way for the ox to draw or carry his burden. He, no doubt, sometimes refitted yokes made by less skillful workmen and made many others for the comfort and usefulness of the oxen.

In later years, Jesus turned His attention to useful work as a healer and teacher. This involved even greater skill in meeting more complex problems than He had faced in the carpenter shop. He needed to understand the basic causes of disease and the cure for these troubles. His teaching involved a clear grasp of great truth, the ability to make that truth clear to others and the faculty of inspiring His listeners to the best in thought and action.

A PRAYER

Lord make me an instrument of Thy peace; where there is hatred, let me sow love; where there is injury, pardon; where there is doubt, faith; where there is despair, hope; where there is darkness, light; and where there is sadness, joy.

O Divine Master, grant that I may not so much seek to be consoled as to console; to be understood, as to understand; to be loved, as to love; for it is in giving that we receive, it is in pardoning that we are pardoned, and it is in dying that we are born to eternal life.

Amen.

—St. Francis of Assisi

To this ministry of healing and teaching, Jesus devoted His unusual talents with great energy and devotion. He was in constant demand by those who sought relief from suffering and were seeking a better understanding of divine truth. His activities involved the period of the day and often also the hours far into the evening. To Him this effort was not burdensome work but a labor of love because He was anxious to enrich the lives of others by alleviating suffering and by inspiring men to nobler living, greater faith in God and fuller dedication of their lives in His service.

143

The Master Workman helps men in many walks of life to see meaning and purpose in their daily toil. In the light of His purpose, they no longer view their daily work as merely a chance to earn a living. It becomes an opportunity to express and develop one's talents, to enrich the lives of others and to serve God.

To the person who is harvesting and manufacturing forest products, this purpose is partcularly evident. These are the materials which provide one's home, his furniture, his newspaper, the magazines which he reads from week to week and the books in his library.

These forest products are also important in the construction of community buildings such as the church, the school, the lodge room, the hospital and other community projects.

The forester who is managing the forests of America is also working in terms of great objectives. He is providing a greater supply of better trees to meet future needs for forest products. He is providing a more constant water supply, greater recreation facilities and more scenes of inspiring beauty.

THE PRAYER LIFE OF JESUS

"Lord Teach us to pray." This was the request of Jesus' disciples as they contrasted the richness of His prayer experience with the shallowness of their own. Of the prayer experiences which these friends and disciples of Jesus observed, the gospel writers have described eleven.

The eleven stories seem to group themselves into three types of experience. The first of these was prayer in the face of great emergency.

In His early ministry, Jesus came to a time of important decision. Previous to this time, His ministry had been of a popular nature. He ministered to the multitudes as He met them along the way. Now the question arose, "Should He supplement this by training some men more intensively to share in His ministry and carry on His work?" If He answered this question in the affirmitive, He had to choose men of insight, noble purpose and courage. He spent a night in prayer, seeking divine wisdom and strength for the choice. Next morning He made His decision known and announced the names of the men who were to be His companions and followers.

Another great life emergency came near the end of life. Following the Lord's supper in the Upper Room of Jerusalem, He went into the Garden of Gethsemane. Leaving His companions, He went into the deeper recesses of the garden. One of them overheard His prayer in the midst of a terrific struggle. The first part of His prayer was, "Heavenly Father, let this cup pass away." As He prayed on, the path of duty became clear. He saw that it led by way of the cross, then offered a much greater prayer, "Nevertheless not My will but Thine be done." With insight concerning the path of duty, there came also courage and strength to walk the way of the cross.

But Jesus' prayer life was not confined to prayer in the face of great emergencies. His longest recorded prayer is one made for others. In this He prayed for His followers and friends. This was a prayer that their lives might be purified and dedicated to the service of God. It was also a great expression of desire for unity among them.

His greatest prayer was one for His enemies. As He hung on the cross and observed the men who had actually been responsible for His hours of agony, He lifted His eyes heavenward and offered the greatest prayer which ever fell from the lips of man, "Father, forgive them for they know not what they do."

Several of Jesus' prayer experiences took the form of quiet meditation. These need to be viewed against the background of the constant demand upon His teaching and healing ministry. Every day He was surrounded by people who wanted their blindness turned into light, their lameness into strength, their illness into health, people who were seeking truth about God and a better way of life.

Under these conditions, Jesus sometimes went out into a quiet spot in the early morning or the late evening to pray.

On one occasion, He spent a day healing and teaching the people at a spot across the Sea of Galilee. That day blind men saw the light of day; lame men walked; sick men were made well. Many people found a new experience of God, forgiveness for their sin, new power to overcome obstacles and a new joy.

At the close of the day, Jesus fed the multitude, then He dismissed them with His blessing. He sent His disciples back across the lake to Capernaum by boat, then, "He went up into a mountain to pray and, when evening was come, was there alone."

This was an opportunity for Jesus to develop the spiritual resources of life, to strengthen the spiritual foundations, to be alone with God, to seek and find new insight, courage and strength.

In Jesus' varied and fruitful prayer experience, his disciples found the way to a richer prayer life. It is full of meaning for us in the modern generation as we seek greater reality and a more vital experience.

A NATION GIVES THANKS

On the fourth Thursday in November the nation will pause to give thanks for the abundant blessings of the year and to recognize God as the Creator of the world, the moulder of human destiny and the source of human blessings.

This observance has its roots in the experience of the early Pilgrims at Plymouth, Massachusetts, who, in spite of severe illness and the loss of more than half of their number during the first winter in New England, set aside a season to thank God for his rich blessings.

These early Pilgrims found their reason for Thanksgiving in a profound religious faith which had led them to a new land with its fresh opportunities and also its hardships and dangers. This faith in God gave them courage, strength and poise in the midst of hardship and sorrow as it had done for the Psalmist in the Old Testament period and for Jesus in the midst of suffering on the Cross.

People of the nation find many reasons for Thanksgiving in this year 1959. This is particularly true of those whose radiant faith, like that of the early Pilgrims, gives them courage and strength in the midst of adversity and sorrow.

Last year we celebrated Thanksgiving day in a period of declining prosperity; this year prosperity has returned in large measure. More men have been employed; demand for the products of the forest has been keener; both workmen and business leaders have found better incomes to sustain themselves and their families. For this increased prosperity we are grateful this year .

But life has many great blessings which endure through periods of prosperity or recession. These include rich friendships and fine associations, a large measure of health and strength, the opportunity of constructive service but also some chance for rest and recreation, opportunities for the enlargement of life's outlook through education, freedom of speech and worship in this land of opportunity.

A PRAYER

O God, the source of every blessing, we thank Thee for Thy continued mercies; for abundant harvests and their contribution to our daily lives, for fine associations and the inspiration they bring, for our daily work and the challenge it offers, for the church of Christ and its opportunity for fellowship in worship and service, for the eternal hills around us which stand as a symbol of creative beauty and divine strength, and for the land in which we live with its great ideals of liberty and brotherhood. Help us to be thankful for all these blessings and to use them wisely for the enrichment of life and the glory of God.

Grant that, like the Pilgrims of earlier times, we may have the courage to endure hardship and the faith to go forward in the face of great adversity, ever mindful of Thy grace and strength in the time of deepest need.

We ask this in Jesus' name.

                              Amen.

We will express our thanks to God for these and other blessings in acts of public worship and also in our private prayers. In doing so, we will make use of poems, hymns and prayers which will help us to more adequately express our thanks and praise. These prayers of thanksgiving will be a part of our life and faith throughout the year as well as on Thanksgiving day.

But we will express our thanks to God even more by the wise use of the blessings which he has given us including our rich forest resources, great friendships and associations, opportunities for both worship and learning and more active citizenship in a great democracy.

LIVING MEMORIALS

The beautiful white birch forest on Route 2 near Shelburne, New Hampshire, was dedicated some year ago as a Memorial Forest in memory of the men who had given their lives in the service of their country. The people of the community felt that only a Living Memorial was appropriate for the occasion.

The beauty of this white birch forest is an inspiration and a constant reminder to citizens of the area and also to those who travel through.

In his well-known address on the battlefield at Gettysburg, Abraham Lincoln expressed a similar view: "It is for us, the living, to be here dedicated to the great task remaining before us—that from these honored dead we take increased devotion to that cause for which they gave the last full measure of devotion; that we here highly resolve that these dead shall not have died in vain; that this nation under God, shall have a new birth of freedom, and that government of the people, by the people and for the people shall not perish from the earth."

President Lincoln believed that a memorial service such as that conducted on the field at Gettysburg was not enough, that the only suitable memorial was an honest effort on the part of American citizens to pursue the objectives and ideals for which these men lived and died.

In many communities throughout the land, we will march in parades and hold memorial services on Memorial Day. These services are appropriate for the occasion and have done much to perpetuate the memories of men's sublime courage and deeds of valor.

But these services will have meaning only as individual citizens perpetuate the memory of men in terms of dedication to the building of a great nation and the promotion of vital democracy in every community throughout the nation. This kind of consecrated effort will provide Living Memorials in terms of a nation's strength and a democratic way of life which is both effective and enduring.

GOD MEETS ME IN THE MOUNTAINS

"God Meets Me in the Mountains
When I climb alone and high;
Up where the tapered spruce
Will guide my glances to the sky.
Somehow I seem to lose him
In the jostle of the street;
But, on a twisty deer trail,
As I trudge along alone,
A mystic presence in the forest
Seems to stay my feet."

These words from the heart and pen of the poet express the experiences and feelings of many of us who live and work in the woods. An awareness of God's presence often comes to us as we travel along the trails, look across the lake upon a scene of beauty or view the surrounding landscape from the top of a rugged mountain.

The writer travelled one winter day along a winding tote road as the snow fell gently upon the spruce and balsam trees along the way. Some distance farther on, the clouds cleared away and the bright sunlight shone down upon the scene where the fresh snow covered these spruce and balsam trees with its blanket of pure white. Quite naturally his thoughts turned to the words of the poet. The presence of the God of beauty seemed very near.

On a clear summer evening the writer flew by plane from the Cedar River flow in the Adirondacks to Lake George. As we flew along at an elevation of 4,000 feet or a little more, the panorama of the whole Adirondacks stretched out underneath and around us. As one looked to the Northward, he saw Mt. Marcy and the more rugged peaks in that area, but his vision also stretched toward the South into the Mohawk Valley. He could look Westward into the Black River Valley and beyond but also to the Eastward to Lake Champlain, Lake George and

A PRAYER

O God, the Creator of the Universe, we thank Thee for warm summer days with the opportunity which they bring for increased logging activity and also outdoor recreation. H e l p us to use these opportunities wisely, with the tools at our disposal, that we might help to enrich the lives of others and to build the resources of the nation.

Give us a deep appreciation of the forests in which we work; of the products which it yields for the enrichment of human life, of the contribution it makes in the control of our water resources, of its opportunities for recreation and its great scenic values. Enable us to guard these resources well and use them wisely for the happiness of people who live in our own and coming generations.

We ask this in Jesus' name.
Amen.

148

into the Green Mountains of Vermont. As one looked upon this scene, he thought of the words of the ancient Psalmist. "The earth is the Lord's and the fullness thereof; the world and they that dwell therein."

On another occasion, the writer stood on the shore of a lake one morning in late September. Not a breath of air seemed to move. The surface of the lake was like a mirror reflecting a scene of great beauty on the other side of the lake where the dark reds of the soft maple, the yellows and the bright reds of other species were mingled with the dark green of the balsam, spruce and pine. The reflection in the water was as clear and vivid as the scene itself, making a scene of indescribable beauty which the observer was able to capture in his movie camera for the inspiration of himself and others on frequent occasions.

On a trip to the top of Mt. Marcy the writer travelled by way of Hanging Speer Falls where the clear waters of the river fall many feet upon a shelf of rock, then tumble down to another shelf of rock and finally take a long tumble to a deep pool at the bottom of the falls.

The beauty and majesty of this secluded waterfalls is a thrilling experience which one never forgets. It is less powerful but much more beautiful than Niagara. It is one of the spots where one feels the presence of the Great Creator who is the Author of all beauty and at the same time the Father of the individual.

DISCOVERY AND REVELATION

This article is being written in a shady spot along Route 120 near Andover, Maine, and about 1/8 mile from the big dome which covers Telstar.

The scene before the writer furnishes a striking contrast between the old and the new, the conservative and the revolutionary. The big Telstar dome, which stands out clearly against the horizon, is partly screened by some stately pine trees whose life reaches back more than a century. These pine trees have looked down upon the people of several passing generations and upon many interesting events, including the logging programs which took most of their contemporaries for the use of an industry, the happiness of people and the growing strength of a nation.

Telstar, on the other hand, is a product of the present, with its major achievements largely in the future. When a sufficient number of satellites have been successfully launched heavenward, international television programs can be carried on continuously. Its effect upon the use of language and international relations may be very profound.

Telstar is a striking illustration of the genius of man. This includes his achievements in scientific research, his ability to organize a cooperative plan in financing the project and the practical scientific discoveries and plans for financing.

The writer believes that it is a more striking demonstration of God's revelation which is the other side of discovery. Revelation includes both the scientist and the prophet. Both are men who are dissatisfied with known truth and life as it is in their time and are constantly seeking to enlarge the horizon. They are seeking to better understand the natural resources of the universe and the resources of human life. It is to men and women of this purpose that God reveals His truth which often breaks suddenly upon the mind in the midst of an earnest search.

IN THY PRESENCE

Lord, what a change within us
  one short hour
Spent in Thy presence will prevail to make!
What heavy burdens from our
  bosoms take,
What parched grounds refresh us
  with a shower!
We kneel, and all around us
  seems to lower;
We rise, and all, the distant and
  the near,
Stands forth in sunny outline
  brave and clear;
We kneel, how weak; we rise,
  how full of power!
Why, therefore, should we do
  ourselves this wrong,
Or others, that we are not always strong,
That we are ever overborne with
  care,
That we should ever weak or
  heartless be,
Anxious or troubled, when with
  us is prayer,
And joy and strength and courage are with Thee!
        —Archbishop Trench.

This type of revelation and discovery would include the early writer who looked out upon the world around him and said, "In the beginning God created the heavens and the earth," Moses at the burning bush and on Mt. Sinai, Isaiah discovering fresh vitality in the act of worship, Columbus discovering a new continent, Walter Reed seeking the cause and cure of yellow fever and many others.

Telstar may also furnish a striking demonstration of the power of prayer. If individuals and groups can communicate with each other in distant areas of the world or space, is prayer unreasonable. Prayer also opens opportunities of communication between the individual and God which needs further exploration.

MULTIPLE USE OF FOREST LAND

The Multiple Use of both private and public forest land is essential for man's welfare and happiness in our time, and for the welfare and happiness of coming generations.

Multiple Use means greater abundance in useful forest products, recreational opportunities, scenic beauty, wildlife and water supply.,

A leader in the fish and game division in New York State's Conservation Department once made this remark about the Adirondacks, "The deer herd will need to get their food in increasing measure on privately-owned forest land." He was aware that the "Adirondack Preserve," with its "Forever Wild" policy, did not provide sufficient food for deer and that the harvesting of timber did improve the deer's food supply.

Advocates of Multiple Use are aware that all the land may not serve all of these purposes at the same time. Some areas may major in one or two uses. Some high land areas such as mountain tops may be largely wilderness.

The forests around some of the more beautiful lakes may have scenic beauty and recreation as their major functions. Here the summer vacationists will find ample opportunities for boating, camping, fishing, hiking, and quiet meditation.

The majority of forest areas will furnish many of these opportunities along with the harvesting of forest products. They will furnish the material for homes, furniture, books, newspapers, magazines, schools and churches; and, at the same time, will furnish better opportunities for hunting and perhaps perform several other of these important functions.

There is evidence of a growing appreciation of these varied uses and values of forest land among private owners of forest land throughout the Northeast, the Central West, the Lake States, and the Appalachian region. The U.S. Forest Service and many of the states are also managing publicly-owned lands on a Multiple Use basis. There is a growing conviction among many foresters and others that this kind of forest is the greatest heritage which we can pass on to coming generations.

ACKNOWLEDGMENTS

For Encouraging the Author to Write the Book—

V. Rev. Msgr. Robert G. Sullivan, Boonville, New York
Howard Thomas, Prospect, New York
Miss Mabel A. Pease, Geneva, New York

For Furnishing Valuable Information—

Paul Aikey, Wanakena, New York
Rev. William J. Burger, Jr., Farmington, Maine
Mrs. Marie Cornell, Campbell, New York
Prof. James F. Dubuar, Earlville, New York
Frank Eldred, Tupper Lake, New York
Mrs. Mary Mason Gordon, Ithaca, New York
R. S. Goodell, Barnum, Minnesota
William Griffin, Star Lake, New York
Mrs. Herman Gurlock, Duluth, Minnesota
Prof. Phillip Haddock, Wanakena, New York
Mrs. Carolyn Hopkins, Woodgate, New York
Mrs. Agnes Atwood Jones, Bradford, Pennsylvania
Dr. Earl Jackman, New York City
Herbert Keith, Wanakena, New York
David MacAleese, Cranberry Lake, New York
Miss Margaret Mason, Danville, New York
Prof. Lucien Plumley, Wanakena, New York
Alexander Ross, Newton Falls, New York
Mrs. Wesley Scheer, Howard Lake, Minnesota
Louis Simmons, Tupper Lake, New York
Clyde and George Sykes, Cranberry Lake, New York

154

Miss Helen Teare, New Providence, New Jersey
The Lumber Camp News, Old Forge, New York
The Northeastern Logger, Old Forge, New York
The Last of the Giants —RIMMER
The Parish of the Pines — (1913) WHITTLES

For Reviewing and Correcting All or Part of Manuscript—

Harold W. Charbonneau, Boonville, New York
William Griffin, Star Lake, New York
Miss Phebe M. King, Scipio Center, New York
Miss Margaret Mason, Danville, New York
Prof. Lucien Plumley, Wanakena, New York
Rev. Frederick G. Reed, Perryville, Kentucky
Mrs. Grace M. Risley, Old Forge, New York
Alexander Ross, Newton Falls, New York
Prof. William Rutherford, Paul Smiths, New York
Mrs. Wesley Scheer, Howard Lake, Minnesota
Howard Thomas, Prospect, New York

For Art Work—

John D. Mahaffy, Boonville, New York

For Typing —

Mrs. Emelia Weaver, Old Forge, New York

> *The author has tried to achieve a high degree of accuracy in the writing of this book. As he concludes it, he is aware that much important information has not been included in it. Such information supplied by readers may provide material for a later edition or another book.*

155